Monster

By Abigail Hood

Published by Playdead Press 2022

© Abigail Hood 2022

Abigail Hood has asserted her rights under the Copyright, Design and Patents Act, 1988, to be identified as the author of this work.

A CIP catalogue record for this book is available from the British Library.

ISBN 978-1-915533-00-5

Playdead Press
www.playdeadpress.com

MONSTER was first performed at the Park Theatre, London on Wednesday 27th July 2022 with the following cast:

CAST

Zoe Douglas	**Caitlin Fielding**
Kayleigh Grey	**Abigail Hood**
Rebecca Hastie	**Emma Keele**
Hazel Grey	**Gillian Kirkpatrick**
John Parker	**Kevin Tomlinson**
Steve Hastie	**Kevin Wathen**

CREATIVES

Director & dramaturg	**Kevin Tomlinson**
Writer	**Abigail Hood**

CAST

Caitlin Fielding | Zoe Douglas
Since graduating from Rose Bruford College, Caitlin's theatre credits have included: *Mr Gillie* (Finborough Theatre); *Macbeth* (Quarter Too Ensemble); *A Midsummer Night's Dream* and *Macbeth* (Young Shakespeare Company).

Her TV / Film credits include: *The Things I See* (BBC) and *A Right Royal Roxy* (Short Film). Commercials include: *Lidl Nachos* (Food Hall).

Abigail Hood | Kayleigh Grey
Since graduating from the Oxford School of Drama, Abigail's theatre credits have included: *That Face* (Royal Court); *Faultlines* (Union); *The Snow Queen* (Scarborough Stephen Joseph); *The Bomb* (Lancaster Dukes); *True Love Waits* (Latitude Festival), *The Lesson Before Break* (Theatre 503); *Weapons of Happiness* (Finborough Theatre); *Romeo and Juliet* (Salisbury Playhouse); *Whispering Happiness* (Box of Tricks); *All The Little Lights* (Derby Theatre); *The Snow Queen* (Pegasus); *Contractions* (Old Fire Station, Oxford); *On The Edge and Crazy Little Thing Called Love* (Kepow Theatre Company - UK Tour); *Bleeding Hearts* (Bolton Octagon); *Dangling* (Southwark Playhouse); *Spiral, The Answer* (Park Theatre); *A Midsummer Night's Dream* (Bard City) and, most recently, *Private Peaceful* (Nottingham Playhouse & Jonathan Church No.1 Tour).

Her TV/Film credits include: *The Bill* (ITV); *The Things I See* (BBC) and *The Lesson* (Urban Fox).

Emma Keele | Rebecca Hastie

Emma trained at LAMDA and the Stella Adler Studio (NY). Theatre credits include: *East is East* (Birmingham Rep & National Theatre); *The Curious Incident of the Dog in the Night-Time* (National Theatre – International Tour); *Abigail's Party* (40th Anniversary  Production, Theatre Royal Bath and UK No.1 Tour); *The End of the Line*, *A Bunch of Amateurs* (Southwold Summer Repertory); *The Borrowers* (Polka Theatre); *Yen* (Gothenburg English Studio Theatre); *April in Paris* (UK No.1 tour); *September in the Rain* (UK No.1 Tour); *Phaedra's Love* (Arcola Theatre).

TV and film credits include: *The Suspect* (ITV, to be aired Autumn 2022); *Emmerdale* (recurring role, ITV); *Silent Witness* (BBC); *Coronation Street*, *Downton Abbey* (ITV); *Doctors*, *New Tricks* (BBC); *Downhill* (Feature), *22. Anna Matthews* (Short, Best Actress Award at Oxford International Film Festival 2021); *Jo* (Short, Best Actress Award at MovieValley Bazza Cinema Fest 2018).

 **Gillian Kirkpatrick** | Hazel Grey

Gillian trained at RSAMD and The Royal Academy of Music. Theatre includes: *Hairspray* (London Coliseum); *Sweeney Todd* (Bergen National Opera); *The Bridges of Madison County* (Menier Chocolate Factory); *Dr Faustess* (Cockpit Theatre); *Skellig* (Nottingham Playhouse); *The Last Ones* (Jermyn Street); *Spring Awakening* (Hope Mill); *Sunny Afternoon* (Harold Pinter); *The House of Mirrors & Hearts* (Arcola); *Happy*

Ending (Arcola); *It's a Wonderful Life* (Bridge House); *American Psycho* (Almeida); *Say It With Flowers* (Sherman Theatre, Cardiff); *Chess* (Union); *Sweeney Todd* (Chichester Festival Theatre & Adelphi); *Hairspray* (Original UK Tour); *Billy Elliot* (Victoria Palace); *Into The Woods* (Royal Opera House); *Blood Brothers* (Phoenix Theatre & UK Tour); *The Fulham Jesus* (Baron's Court); *Fear of Trees* (Old Red Lion); *Carmen* (New Vic, Stoke and Tour); *Sweeney Todd* and *Paradise Moscow* (Opera North); *A Tale of Two Cities* (Birmingham Alexandra); *I Love You You're Perfect Now Change* (Comedy Theatre); *The Rink* (Orange Tree); *Company* (Manchester Library); *Me & My Girl* and *My Cousin Rachel* (Perth Rep); *Macbeth* (German Tour).

TV and Film includes: *Dorcha (The Darkness)* (Tharun Productions); *Inside Balmoral* (Ch5); *Eastenders* (BBC); *Holby City* (BBC); *River City* (BBC Scotland); *The Bird* (Segalovich Prods); *Distant Voices* (Film Oxford); *Nothing in the Middle* (NFTS / BFI); *Emmi* (Film Oxford / Fernie Films).

Kevin Tomlinson | John Parker
Kevin trained with Jacques Lecoq, Philippe Gaulier and on the Acting Course at Middlesex University. Theatre credits include, three previous productions at the Park Theatre; *Spiral*, *Beneath the Blue Rinse* and *The Answer*. Other credits include: *The Ragged Child* (Royal and Derngate Theatre, Northampton); *Flat 73* (Cheltenham Everyman Theatre / UK tour); *Whose Story Is It Anyway?* (Theatre Royal, Bury St Edmunds); *Facing It Out* (Told by an Idiot, BAC);

Ramblin Rose (Royal and Derngate Theatre, Northampton); *Madame Tellier's Establishment* (Trestle TC, Brighton Gardner AC); *Seven Ages* (Stephen Joseph Theatre, Scarborough / UK tour); *On The Edge!* (York Theatre Royal / UK tour).

Kevin has worked with the legendary Keith Johnstone (author of *Impro*) on numerous occasions, taking the lead role in several of his plays including *Damian* and *The Invitation*. Kevin also performed alongside the cast of *Whose Line is It Anyway?* at the Hackney Empire, in a fundraiser for the Royal Court Theatre (directed by Phellim McDermott and Keith Johnstone).

Film credits include: John Duncan in *Devil's Harvest*, alongside Brian Blessed and Julie T. Wallace. TV credits include: Puck in *A Midsummer Night's Dream* for BBC2 Open University.

Kevin Wathen | Steve Hastie
Kevin trained at Drama Centre London, graduating in 2001. Kevin is also a musician and producer, producing music for film and upcoming artists.

Theatre includes: *The Last Ship*, (Northern Stage / National Tour / The Princess of Wales Theatre, Toronto); *The Season Ticket, Get Carter* (Northern Stage); *McQueen* (Theatre Royal Haymarket); *What Falls Apart* (Live Theatre, Newcastle); *Crocodiles* (Manchester Royal Exchange); *Billy Elliot* (Victoria Palace); *Quadrophenia* (Plymouth Theatre Royal / National Tour); *Breakfast With Johnny Wilkinson* (Menier Chocolate Factory); *Hair* (The Gate Theatre); *Alice's Adventures In Wonderland* (Bristol Old Vic); *Hamlet* (Old Vic); *Skellig* (Young Vic).

Television includes: *Vera* (ITV); *Doctors* (BBC); *George Gently* (BBC); *Blue Murder* (ITV); *Holby City* (BBC); *Silent Witness* (BBC); *The Bill* (ITV); *Judge John Deed* (BBC).

Film Includes: *Strike, The Universal* (My Life Films); *Regional Sales Manager* (Blink Productions); *Care* (Warp Films/Sky Arts); *This Damnation; And Kill Them* (Channel 4 Coming Up Series).

CREATIVE

Kevin Tomlinson | Director / Dramaturg
Kevin is the artistic director of KEPOW Theatre Company and past winner of the Rose Bruford Trust Directors Award. He has directed 45 plays professionally, including several plays for the British Council in Singapore and numerous other productions in Hong Kong and Dubai. For six years he was a regular contributor to the work of the Royal National Theatre in London; teaching acting workshops in the Studio and working as the comedy consultant on the Education Department's touring production of *A Midsummer Night's Dream*.

Kevin has worked with the legendary Keith Johnstone (author of *Impro*) on numerous occasions – in Canada and the UK – directing several world premieres of Keith's plays; most notably the highly successful sell-out production of *Open Season* in Calgary in 2007. Over the last 20 years, Kevin has directed and taught in New Zealand, America, South Korea, Norway, Germany, Holland, UAE, France, Bali, Hawaii and Hong Kong, not to mention at many top UK drama schools. During Lockdown, Kevin directed *Measure for Measure* and *Tartuffe* at DSL with their graduating students, and a full mask production of *Animal Farm* at the Oxford Pegasus Theatre.

For two years, Kevin was the writer-in-residence at the Royal and Derngate Theatre in Northampton. His play *Who?* was performed upstairs at the Royal Court Theatre in London, having won the Sunday Times Playwright Award. Due to his past writing experience, Kevin also works as a dramaturg.

Abigail Hood | Writer

Abigail's previous credits include *Dangling* (Southwark Playhouse); *Spiral* (Park Theatre) and *Atlantis* (Old Fire Station, Oxford). She is very excited to be bringing her brand new play *Monster* to the Park.

Ricky McFadden | Stage Manager

Ricky trained at the Academy of Live and Recorded Arts on the Stage Management and Technical Theatre course.

His most recent Stage Management credits include Company Stage Manager for *Tony! [The Tony Blair Rock Opera]* (Park200, Park Theatre); Stage Manager / Relighter for *An Evening of Eric n Ern* (England and Wales Tour) and Stage Manager for *Pippin* (Charing Cross Theatre).

Other Stage Management credits include Company Stage Manager for *La Cage Aux Folles [The Play]*; *Sydney and the Old Girl*; *Whodunnit [Unrehearsed]* and *Rosenbaum's Rescue* (all Park200, Park Theatre); Deputy Stage Manager for *Red Riding Hood [The Rock n Roll Panto]* (Mack Theatre, Mountview) and Company Stage Manager for Episodes 1-6 of *The Theatre Channel* (web series).

ABOUT VERITAS THEATRE COMPANY

Veritas is a UK based theatre company specialising in challenging and provocative new writing. The company seeks to give a voice to new British writers who have something to say about the world we live in today. The themes and actions within these new plays may be highly amusing or highly disturbing, but - either way - are always based on a desire to tell the truth as the writer sees it. Hence the name of the company: Veritas (the goddess of truth in Roman mythology).

ABOUT KEPOW THEATRE COMPANY

Kepow are an Oxford based theatre company committed to creating innovative, exciting, dynamic theatre that appeals to a wide demographic. Their shows involve a combination of comedy, pathos, improvisation and mask work.

Since 2003, Kepow's shows have toured internationally to 14 countries on 4 continents, including: New Zealand, Canada, Hong Kong, Singapore, South Korea, Germany, Norway, Bali, Hawaii, UAE, France and Holland.

They have won a "*clutch of awards*" (The Independent on Sunday). These include the Sunday Times Playwright Award and Rose Bruford Trust Directors Award.

A NOTE FROM THE WRITER

Guilt. We've all felt it. The discomfort in the pit of the stomach, the inability to sleep, the nagging insistent thoughts that prevent enjoyment of anything else. But what if you had committed the ultimate sin? How would you go on living? Particularly if this act was committed during your childhood? Is it fair or right that a murderer can go on to create another life? How does a bereaved parent ever come to terms with the loss of a child at the hands of another child? Can they, should they, ever forgive?

I wrote *Monster* in response to these questions in the summer of 2020 during Lockdown. I found myself undertaking extensive research into the lives of various minors whose abhorrent acts of violence have shocked the world. *Monster* is the result. The play doesn't provide any easy answers, but it does seek to provoke debate; in the process, exploring the themes of guilt, blame, violence and redemption.

Monster asks: are people born evil, or do they become evil as a result of their upbringing? Is it possible to prevent someone becoming the worst possible version of themselves and avert the devastation they inflict upon others? Can we prevent such things from happening or are we, as a society, failing our young people? *Monster* asks these questions in the hope that other families can be spared the grief inflicted upon them by such acts and save the children who commit them from themselves. The play is by no means a comfortable watch / read, but I hope it proves to be a stimulating one nonetheless.

Abi Hood | Writer

A NOTE FROM THE DRAMATURG / DIRECTOR

On reading the first draft of *Monster*, I was struck by the power of Abi's writing: it's sparse, snappy dialogue (sometimes darkly humorous, sometimes bitingly cruel); the wonderful forward thrust of the narrative with its surprising twists and turns, and the emotionally engaging characters, going through life events we would all hate to experience ourselves. All of Abi's strengths as a writer were there to see and I felt a wonderful play was beginning to emerge; intense, entertaining, naughty and, at times, emotionally challenging. Like a sculptor, chiselling away at a block of stone and slowly creating a work of art, Abi was creating what I felt was a potentially powerful piece of new writing, tackling important issues that plague our society and other societies around the world. In the months that followed, we worked together to make the script as lean as possible: jettisoning two characters and 30% of the dialogue; ironing out inconsistences; and focusing on character 'arcs' and subtext.

The end result, I hope you'll agree, is a punchy, provocative play, that has humour, pathos and dramatic tension vying for supremacy. The themes are dark. The characters complex and complicated. There are no easy solutions to the questions Abi raises, but the play does offer some hope, despite the plays ominous title and the shocking events within the narrative. This is a play that needs to be seen, read and discussed by many people. The themes within it are of vital importance. We need to explore them, collectively, as a society. What are the causes of violent action? How should we treat juvenile criminals? How does one cope after the loss of a loved one? These questions - and more besides - need to be discussed by as many people as possible. For only together, through shared discussion, followed by action, can we hope to tackle the underlying causes that lead to the creation of 'monsters'.

Kevin Tomlinson | Dramaturg & Director
Artistic Director, Kepow Theatre

ABOUT PARK THEATRE

Park Theatre was founded by Artistic Director, Jez Bond and Creative Director Emeritus, Melli Marie. The building opened in May 2013 and, with four West End transfers, two National Theatre transfers and 13 national tours in its first nine years, quickly garnered a reputation as a key player in the London theatrical scene. Park Theatre has received six Olivier nominations, won numerous Off West End Offie Awards, and won The Stage's Fringe Theatre of the Year and Accessible Theatre Award.

Park Theatre is an inviting and accessible venue, delivering work of exceptional calibre in the heart of Finsbury Park. We work with writers, directors and designers of the highest quality to present compelling, exciting and beautifully told stories across our two intimate spaces.

Our programme encompasses a broad range of work from classics to revivals with a healthy dose of new writing, producing in-house as well as working in partnership with emerging and established producers. We strive to play our part within the UK's theatre ecology by offering mentoring, support and opportunities to artists and producers within a professional theatre-making environment.

Our Creative Learning strategy seeks to widen the number and range of people who participate in theatre, and provides opportunities for those with little or no prior contact with the arts.

In everything we do we aim to be warm and inclusive; a safe, welcoming and wonderful space in which to work, create and visit.

★★★★★ "A five-star neighbourhood theatre." Independent

As a registered charity [number 1137223] with no public subsidy, we rely on the kind support of our donors and volunteers. To find out how you can get involved visit parktheatre.co.uk

With special thanks to:

Richard Prouse, Natasha Hancock, Renata Allen, PJ, Kara Young, Gill and Jerry Hood, Holly-Rose Tomlinson, Jude Thorp, Nomi Everall, Lucy Turner and the Kathryn Turner Trust, Vanessa Clarke, Jordan Taylor Allen, and Pollyanna Knight

For Mum and Dad – because you are an inspiration and never stop believing in me

CHARACTERS (in order of appearance)

Kayleigh Grey *14 / 30, daughter of Hazel*

Zoe Douglas *14 / 30, best friend of Kayleigh*

Rebecca Hastie *33 / 46, wife of Steve*

Hazel Grey *45 / 58, mother of Kayleigh*

Steve Hastie *34 / 47, husband of Rebecca*

Rosie Hastie *5.5 / 9 weeks, daughter of Rebecca and Steve*

John Parker *32, husband of Kayleigh*

Phoebe Parker *11 days, daughter of Kayleigh and John*

Act 2 begins just over twelve and a half years after Act 1 finishes. The characters should be played by the same actors throughout. Act 1 takes place in a variety of locations in and around Drumchapel, Glasgow in 2006.

Act 2 takes place in a variety of locations in Scotland between 2019-2022.

A forward slash in the dialogue (/) indicates that the next actor should start their line, creating overlapping speech.

ACT 1 SCENE 1

2006. Mid-April. 4.30pm. A wasteland in Drumchapel,
Glasgow. ZOE, 14, dressed in school uniform, sits inside a
concrete pipe. We don't see her, just smoke coming from within.
KAY, 14, enters in a dishevelled school uniform, sees the smoke
and smirks

KAY: (*into the pipe*) Boo

ZOE starts

ZOE: Oi, what you being a dick for?

KAY laughs

KAY: Give us one

A cigarette is thrown out of the pipe followed by a lighter, KAY
lights it, smokes

                You weren't in school this afternoon

ZOE: How'd you know?

KAY: Came to spy on you in Science. After I got
                sent home

ZOE: Can't believe you're in trouble
                again. Everyone was talking about it

KAY: Was just a scuffle. I didn'ae even draw blood

ZOE: Someone said you tried to rip out her nose
                ring

KAY: I wouldn'ae do that

ZOE:	Course you would'nae *(giggles)*
KAY:	She's had that nose ring since S1
ZOE:	I know. Donna-Mc-Tit-Face without a nose ring is like…
KAY:	Cock without balls

ZOE laughs

ZOE:	Why d'you do it?
KAY:	The usual. She was being a twat. About you. *(Beat)* What you doing?
ZOE:	What's it look like? *(beat)* Sitting in a pipe
KAY:	Right
ZOE:	I only missed last lesson… biology, cutting up frogs
KAY:	Best bit
ZOE:	It's gross
KAY:	I like it when they twitch. When you hit a tendon

ZOE makes a gagging sound

	You coming out or what?
ZOE:	Or what. Can't
KAY:	Why?
ZOE:	Got my period didn't I?

KAY:	So?
ZOE:	Went everywhere.
KAY:	No!
ZOE:	Left a fuck off bloody smudge on the stool
KAY:	Anyone see?
ZOE:	Tracy fuckin' Watson
KAY:	Shit. What she say?
ZOE:	Nothing she just pulled this face like I'd shat on her shoes
KAY:	Fuck
ZOE:	And Mr Conway
KAY:	Nooooooo (*laughs*) At least he'll know you're a woman

Beat

	So what you gonna do? Wait 'til it's dark?
ZOE:	Yeah
KAY:	Don't be a twat
ZOE:	Just leave it
KAY:	Come out
ZOE:	No
KAY:	I said come out

21

Silence

I'll block off your air supply

KAY takes her jumper off and secures it over one end of the pipe.
ZOE appears from the other

ZOE: You know I'm claustrophobic

KAY: Wanted to see your pretty face... (*seeing the*
                  blood stain on ZOE's trousers) shit

ZOE: I know

KAY: That's disgusting (*she starts to laugh*

ZOE: Fuck off

KAY: Take this

She ties her jumper around ZOE's waist

                  Never know now

Beat

KAY: I like watching it come out. Great globules of
                  womb wall. Like syrup

ZOE: Stop it

KAY smiles

KAY: He'll still want to fuck you

ZOE: Who?

KAY: The frog dissector

22

ZOE:	Mr Conway?
KAY:	Yeah
ZOE:	Probably does, dirty bastard
KAY:	You'd love it though (*she simulates thrusting and impersonates Mr Conway*) "The (*she thrusts*) inner (*she thrusts*) lining (*she thrusts*) of (*she thrusts*) the (*she thrusts*) uterus" (*she thrusts*)
ZOE:	(*repulsed*) You're a fuckin' skank
KAY:	Tell me I'm wrong
ZOE:	You're wrong
KAY:	You love cock though
ZOE:	Yeah
KAY:	I always want to bite them. Do y' know what I mean?
ZOE:	Um
KAY:	When they're deep down your throat and your teeth are at the very base
ZOE:	That's fucked up
KAY:	I know. I wouldn't actually do it, your mouth would be filled with their cock blood, it'd go everywhere and what would you do with the cock?
ZOE:	Stop it

KAY: It's just a thought I have. I have it every time. I love that feeling. I could bite off their cock.

ZOE: Can you hear yourself?

KAY laughs

KAY: Miss Hastie says I've got no filter

ZOE: She's right

KAY: Bet you have filthy thoughts

ZOE smiles, coy

About Jack Harvey

ZOE says nothing

You know he's older

ZOE: I know, nineteen and fit as fuck

KAY: He's the cleaner?!

ZOE: So?

KAY: Stinks of bleach

ZOE: Better than shit

KAY laughs

Only when he's cleaning

KAY: Do you imagine doing it at school... in the cleaning cupboard, surrounded by cleaning fluids and toilet roll

ZOE: Stop it

KAY: I bet he's got a long, thin, smooth one, not
                much hair

ZOE: I'm not listening

KAY: Maybe Mr. Conway would come in and find
                you... ask to join in. I bet he's got a fat one

ZOE: To go with his fat belly

KAY: And man boobs

ZOE: Bigger than yours

KAY: Cheeky fucker

KAY grabs ZOE's breasts

ZOE: Oi, what you doing?

KAY: Wanna know what big ones feel like

ZOE: Perv

KAY: Go on, let me. Thought we were mates

ZOE sticks her chest out. KAY carefully touches them

                Heavy, full... water bombs

ZOE: (*pulls away*) That's enough

Beat

                Feel weird now

KAY: Why?

ZOE:	'Cos what you just did
KAY:	'Cos you liked it?
ZOE:	I didn't say that
KAY:	Didn't need to. I saw your pupils dilate
ZOE:	Fuck off
KAY:	I love all that
ZOE:	All what?
KAY:	All that science stuff. Like how your body does things but it's not a choice. Like men getting erections. Like chickens running around when they've had their heads chopped off
ZOE:	What?
KAY:	Happened to a human – a sailor
ZOE:	A sailor?
KAY:	Aye. Had a quarter of his head chopped off, by a bridge or something, just above his eye
ZOE:	Urrrrgggghh
KAY:	In hospital, when they were bandaging his massive wound – sure he was gonna die – he suddenly got up, started walking around… with the top of his head missing
ZOE:	How do you know this stuff?

KAY:	Read it in a book
ZOE:	(*laughs*) You're properly clever
KAY:	I'm not, I just like facts
ZOE:	Wish I was like you
KAY:	You don't
ZOE:	I do. You don't give a fuck. I'd love to be like that.
KAY:	So stop caring
ZOE:	Can't
KAY:	Course you can. Right, next person to walk past them houses, show 'em your tits
ZOE:	I can't
KAY:	You could if you didn'ae care
ZOE:	What if they tell my Mum?
KAY:	They won't see your face! Fuckin hell. Alright, put this over your head.

KAY takes the jumper from ZOE's waist and lobs it over her head

ZOE:	What are you-?
KAY:	Now, now, NOW

ZOE lifts her top squealing as she does it. KAY laughs

Oh my God, he's coming over

ZOE:	Shit, shit, shit

ZOE pulls her top down, scrabbles with the jumper and tries to get back in the pipe. KAY is in hysterics

KAY:	I'm kidding, I don't think he even saw
ZOE:	Oh my God
KAY:	See, fun isn't it?
ZOE:	(*laughing*) You're a fucking headcase
KAY:	I know. So are you
ZOE:	I know. And I DON'T GIVE A FUCK
KAY:	Alright calm down. Don't want someone calling the police

They laugh, calm down. ZOE re-ties jumper around her waist. Silence

Be quite fun to be on the run though

ZOE giggles

Always one step ahead, that'd be us

Beat. She looks at ZOE

We should just fuck off

ZOE:	(*smiles*) Aye. To the Isle of Muck
KAY:	That's right. And ride the wild horses
ZOE:	Tame them

KAY:	No. Be wild wi' em
ZOE:	And how will we live?
KAY:	We'll be savages
ZOE:	Tell me how again?
KAY:	We'll eat carrots and dig holes if it rains
ZOE:	And sleep with the horses for warmth
KAY:	Aye. And no-one will ever come looking because who lives with horses?
ZOE:	Who the fuck?
KAY:	And we'll never be found. We will poof... into thin air

KAY smiles. Beat

ZOE:	I stink
KAY:	Yeah
ZOE:	My Mum'll go ape shit.
KAY:	Is that Miss Hastie?
ZOE:	Fuck off
KAY:	I'm serious
ZOE:	(*looks*) Where? (*Sees her*) Oh shit. Do you think she saw my tits?
KAY:	(*relishing her anxiety*) Mibee

ZOE: I should go

KAY: Just stay for a bit

ZOE: No, I've gott'ae get back, the little ones'll be needin' their tea

KAY: Come back later, stay at mine tonight

ZOE: No

KAY: We can go back late, when she's asleep

ZOE: Mibee another time

KAY: Whatever, come or don't come, I don't give a shit

ZOE: Yes you do

KAY: What?

ZOE: You heard

KAY: Slit tease

REBECCA, 33, enters

Miss

ZOE: Miss

REBECCA: Kay, Zoe

REBECCA sits on a pipe. She is heavily pregnant

KAY: Risky

REBECCA is silent

KAY:	I didn'ae think you liked us nae more
REBECCA:	I needed some fresh air
KAY:	Is that a metaphor? (*To ZOE*) It is. S'what she says when she's had an argument wi' Steve

REBECCA shoots at look at KAY

ZOE:	How long til it's born?
REBECCA:	Four weeks
ZOE:	Can I touch?
REBECCA:	Yeah. It's on the move today

ZOE touches her belly very gently, smiles

ZOE:	Are you getting cramps?
REBECCA:	Sometimes
KAY:	Fucking hell, call the sodding midwife
ZOE:	If you get cramps you should sit in a bath and drink lots of water
REBECCA:	(*smiles*) I'll do that
KAY:	Why don't you examine her as well? Get your head between her thighs
ZOE:	Stop it / Kay
KAY:	/ Is that what you'd like? Eh? The smell of / her

REBECCA: / Enough, Kayleigh. Enough

KAY smirks. There is an awkward silence

ZOE: I should go

KAY: You can't, Miss isn'ae allowed to be alone with me. Isn't that right?

REBECCA: That's what I'm told

ZOE: Sorry Kay, I've got nae choice

REBECCA: It's fine Zoe

ZOE: She'll no' bite you again, will you Kay?

KAY: Depends, if she wants me to or not

ZOE: Kay

KAY: I'm only playing, I'll no' go near her. I swear

ZOE: I'll see you tomorrow. Night Miss

REBECCA: Night

ZOE exits

KAY: I must be made of Velcro 'cos you definitely shouldn'ae be here

REBECCA: Don't do that

KAY: What?

REBECCA: Reduce my life like that

KAY: I /

REBECCA:	/ I told you things in confidence
KAY:	/ Right

Beat

REBECCA:	You like her
KAY:	Yeah
REBECCA:	So don't make her jealous
KAY:	Why should she be jealous?
REBECCA:	She shouldn't
KAY:	Is Steve?
REBECCA:	No
KAY:	(*raising her eyebrows*) I mean a bite on the neck. Usually sexually motivated
REBECCA:	Yeah, but it wasn't and you know it

KAY smirks

KAY:	So you're no' here cos you fancy us then?
REBECCA:	(*not rising to the bait*) I'm here 'cos I heard what you did
KAY:	Donna?

REBECCA nods

It was a fight, it wasn'ae one-way

REBECCA:	You've got to control yourself Kay

KAY:	Why should I?
REBECCA:	You almost ripped her nostril in half
KAY:	She deserved it. It's every fucking day
REBECCA:	That's not the point
KAY:	Zoe's too nice to say anythin'
REBECCA:	I know
KAY:	But I'm no'. You know her.
REBECCA:	Yes I do
KAY:	Do you like her?
REBECCA:	Wouldn't be professional of me to comment
KAY:	Which means no
REBECCA:	I didn't / say that
KAY:	/ I'm like Che Guevara. I'm a revolutionary fighting for the underdog
REBECCA:	You know he ended up being shot
KAY:	Aye. But Donna Mc-tit-face hasn'ae got a gun
REBECCA:	I'm serious Kay, control your temper
KAY:	Is this a bollocking?
REBECCA:	Yes
KAY:	Why do you bother?

REBECCA: Because I care

KAY: I'm dangerous

REBECCA: Are you?

KAY: I took a chunk out of your neck

REBECCA: You were upset

KAY: I get upset a lot

REBECCA: Maybe I think you're worth the risk

KAY: Do you?

REBECCA: I'm here

KAY: I could get you fired

REBECCA: I kn / ow

KAY: / So why? If you don't want to shag us?

REBECCA: Not everything's about sex

KAY: Is it no'? (*beat*) You in love wi' us then?

REBECCA: No. I just care

They sit. Moments pass. KAY takes out a cigarette

KAY: Cheeky drag?

REBECCA: Don't tempt me

KAY: Blessed is the man that endureth temptation: for when he is tried he shall receive the crown of life

REBECCA: I'll look forward to that then

KAY: (*smoking with relish*) Better to reign in Hell, than to serve in Heaven, I say

REBECCA: You're a smart girl Kayleigh Grey

KAY: Because I can quote Milton?

REBECCA: Because of lots of things

Beat

Is someone hurting you?

KAY: (*momentarily thrown*) Other than Donna Mc-tit-face?

REBECCA: Donna Mc-tit-face doesn't use her fists or she'd break her nails

REBECCA waits. KAY is silent

You've got another bruise?

REBECCA reaches toward KAY's face

KAY: I wouldn'ae do that Miss, anyone sees...

REBECCA: (*pointing to the bruise under KAY's eye*) There

KAY: I'm a peach

REBECCA raises her eyebrows

Was a door

REBECCA: I can help you, if you need

KAY:	Good to know
REBECCA:	If there's something
KAY:	What?
REBECCA:	Why do you think I didn't press charges for what you did?
KAY:	'Cos you know I'd break both your legs
REBECCA:	No you wouldn't. You were upset that night because something had happened.
KAY:	Is that right?
REBECCA:	You weren't angry with me
KAY:	Fuckin' hell, you swallowed a psychology book?
REBECCA:	I've been there Kay
KAY:	Where's that?
REBECCA:	Where you are. Where things happen beyond your control and the fear sends you crazy
KAY:	Fuck off Hastie

REBECCA nods, gets up

REBECCA: You're right, I should get going

KAY remains. REBECCA stands and picks up her bag, gives KAY a small, tight smile

KAY: Right. So that's it then?

REBECCA nods

Are you pissed off?

REBECCA: (*shakes her head*) No

KAY: Well what do you expect when you start talking like a twat?

REBECCA: Right. Sorry

REBECCA almost leaves but stops. She turns to KAY

I went to a clinic. I was only eleven weeks pregnant so the procedure could be done without anaesthetic. Ten minutes and it would have been gone. I'd booked the appointment for a Thursday afternoon. I had a free period last lesson, so I knew no-one would miss me. I wouldn't have to tell any lies about where I was. (*beat*) I'd put my phone on silent, so I didn't hear when the hospital rang, or when the school rang or when Dad rang. It was only when I was undressing and the phone fell out of my pocket that I saw the missed calls. My mother had suffered a brain embolism. I left, obviously, went straight there. But it was too late. (*Beat*) Steve was there before me, he didn't ask where I'd been, just held my hand. And I knew right then I was going to have my baby. That Mum dying at that exact moment had to mean something. So as we sat in the hospital café drinking shit coffee,

waiting for Dad to say goodbye, I told Steve
I was pregnant. (*Beat*) I vowed I'd never tell
anyone about the clinic

REBECCA looks at KAY

KAY: Then why you telling me?

REBECCA: So you know what trust is.

A moment. REBECCA leaves

SCENE 2

*Just after 5pm the same day. HAZEL's run-down flat. HAZEL,
45, sits at a table in the half light. She is dressed provocatively
and her face is made-up. She pours herself a shot of whiskey.
KAY enters.*

HAZEL:	You're late.
KAY:	I know
HAZEL:	It's gone five
KAY:	Sorry
HAZEL:	Are you?
KAY:	Yeah
HAZEL:	I'm going out tonight
KAY:	I forgot
HAZEL:	Did you?
KAY:	That's what I said
HAZEL:	I text you
KAY:	Didn't see it
HAZEL:	Lily needs looking after
KAY:	What's she doing here?
HAZEL:	Come for a visit
KAY:	On a school night?

HAZEL:	I didn'ae ask nae questions
KAY:	Scraping the barrel leaving her wi' you

Beat

	Well I'm here now so why don't you fuck off?
HAZEL:	I saw you with that teacher again
KAY:	What of it?
HAZEL:	Breaking the rules
KAY:	What is it to you?
HAZEL:	(*ruffled*) What you doing with her?
KAY:	Nothing
HAZEL:	(*laughs*) Nothing?
KAY:	Talking
HAZEL:	About what?
KAY:	None of your business
HAZEL:	IT IS MA' BUSINESS BECAUSE YOU'RE UNDER MA' ROOF. What have you done to me this time?
KAY:	I've told her nothing. Alright.
HAZEL:	Does she know about this? (*She pulls back her sleeve to reveal a mangled arm*)
KAY:	Stop it

41

HAZEL: That I have to defend myself in my own home

KAY: If I told her that I'd tell her why

Beat

HAZEL: But you would'nae do that would you?

KAY: Dunno

HAZEL: Because it would be your word against mine. And you've got form. You're on record. Can't control yourself

KAY: I've got scars too

HAZEL: Aye, but no witnesses. I've never hurt anyone that didn'ae ask for it

KAY: Or pay for it

HAZEL: To put food in your belly

KAY: And drink down your throat

HAZEL: You're no better than me

KAY: Yes I am

HAZEL: Is that right? Don't kid yourself. This is your lot, same as it is mine

KAY: But mibee it's no', cos I didn'ae choose it

HAZEL: No-one chooses it

KAY: You did

HAZEL:	You really think I want to be like this? That I wouldn'ae rather be livin' in one of them fancy houses in Scotstoun, wi' a husband who brings home a salary, and a secretarial job three days a week in a nice office, where my only problem is being groped by my boss?
KAY:	But why do I have to do it?
HAZEL:	Because I'm getting old and you're ma' big girl
KAY:	But I wasn'ae
HAZEL:	You knew no better then, so where was the harm?
KAY:	The harm? Where was the harm? I came out of your womb with a dick down ma' throat
HAZEL:	You think you deserve better? She's donea job on you hasn't she? You just wait 'til that baby's born. Then you'll see you're nothing to her, not really. Just a five minute flash in the pan to make her feel better about herself. It's only me you can really rely on.
KAY:	Then I'm truly fucked
HAZEL:	You're a spiteful creature Kayleigh Grey
KAY:	Aye. 'S what you made me
HAZEL:	Why do you do this to me? Tie me up in knots.

KAY: (*chanting*) There was an old woman who lived in a shoe,

HAZEL: Stop it

KAY: She had so many children, she didn'ae know what to do,

HAZEL: (*becoming emotional*) As God is my judge I try ma' best

KAY: She gave them some broth without any bread

HAZEL: I'm warning you

KAY: And whipped them all soundly and put them / to bed

HAZEL: / I SAID ENOUGH. You drive me to it

KAY: Is that right?

HAZEL: Whoever spares the rod hates his son, but he who loves him is diligent to discipline him.

KAY: For ma' own good

HAZEL: When you're wild and I've to defend maself

KAY: And what about when you're wild?

HAZEL: Honour your father and your mother, as the Lord your God commanded you

KAY: And this God, he doesn'ae see what else you do?

HAZEL: Get me ma pills

KAY fetches them, HAZEL tips out two and swallows them down quickly

KAY: Do you think God will forgive you?

HAZEL: He sees what I've to put up with

A bang on the door

I'll be back in an hour

HAZEL exits. KAY sits, swigs from the bottle on the table. Moments pass. The door re-opens, HAZEL enters, throws a key on to the floor. KAY looks at it.

He's waiting by the shed

KAY: No

HAZEL: It's you he wants

KAY: No

HAZEL: Fine (*she calls*) Lily

KAY: You bitch

KAY grabs the key and makes to leave. HAZEL stops her and hands her a wine bottle

HAZEL: He wants to use this

KAY winces, braces herself and exits.

SCENE 3

Same day. 5.30pm. STEVE and REBECCA's lounge.
STEVE, 34, stands painting at a large canvas, sheets cover the
floor to protect the carpet. The door slams

REBECCA: (*off*) Hello

STEVE: In here

REBECCA enters

                        Nice walk?

REBECCA: Yeah

STEVE: Long one

REBECCA: Popped to the shop

STEVE: Dairy milk?

REBECCA smiles

                        That's not a craving you know, it's an
                        addiction

REBECCA: It likes it

STEVE: Does it now?

REBECCA: (*nods*) Yeah

STEVE raises his eyebrows, smiles

                        How's it going?

STEVE: I can't get the light right

REBECCA:	(*looks, takes her time*) It' / s
STEVE:	/ No bullshit
REBECCA:	I can see what you mean
STEVE:	(*he sighs*) Knew it
REBECCA:	Sorry
STEVE:	No
REBECCA:	(*cheeky*) Not going to paint us in?

STEVE looks at her, raises his eyebrows

> Which dune was it?

STEVE:	(*shakes his head*) If that's what you want

They laugh. Beat

> You look tired

REBECCA:	I am
STEVE:	Come on

STEVE plumps the cushions for her to sit down

> Drink?

REBECCA:	Wine?
STEVE:	Tea? Kettle's just boiled
REBECCA:	S'pose
STEVE:	Green?

REBECCA moans, sits back, closes her eyes. STEVE leans over,
kisses her

Have you been smoking?

REBECCA: No

He leans in, smells her again

(*half-playful / half-defensive*) Oi (*beat*) I
wouldn't

He nods, smiles, exits to get the tea. REBECCA smells her hair,
sits back, thinks

Do you remember when we first tried to have
sex?

STEVE: (*from off, taken aback*) Um...

REBECCA: And I couldn't relax enough for you to enter
me

STEVE returns with the tea

STEVE: Where's this going?

REBECCA: Even though I really wanted to, the muscles
just seized up. I said it must be 'cos I was
nervous and you said it was fine. The next
time we tried I drank a bottle of red wine
beforehand. But it didn't help. And after the
third time of trying you asked if it was you. I
said no, it definitely wasn't that. And you
said I could trust you, if it was something
else. I said I didn't know what you were
talking about and we didn't speak for three

weeks (*beat*) Then on my birthday I came to your halls of residence and told you what had happened to me

STEVE: Why are you telling me this like I don't know?

REBECCA: 'Cos I want you to remember

STEVE: I do.

REBECCA: No. I want you to remember how hard it was for me to tell you

STEVE: Course I remember

REBECCA: How it was so hard I nearly let you walk away

Beat

I've been with Kay

He breathes heavily

Please don't be angry

STEVE: I'm not

REBECCA: I need you to understand

STEVE: You've been warned Bec

REBECCA: I know

STEVE: She's dangerous

REBECCA: Not really

STEVE: Becca

REBECCA: The violence keeps people away

STEVE: Except you

REBECCA: But when you get past it

STEVE: What?

REBECCA: There's more to her

STEVE: Is there?

REBECCA: I just need time

STEVE: And what if it turns out she's just got a temper?

REBECCA: It's more than that

STEVE: So report your concerns, whatever, the proper channels

REBECCA: She doesn't want that

STEVE: Then leave her alone

REBECCA: How can I?

STEVE: You got help

REBECCA: It was different for me

STEVE: So you don't know how to handle her

REBECCA: She likes me

STEVE: And that's why last time you came home bleeding

REBECCA: She was upset

STEVE: Can you hear what you're saying?

REBECCA: (*breathes heavily*) Yes

STEVE: She's been expelled from two schools and arrested three times for Christ's sake (*beat*) She must be on lists, social services, they must know more than you?

REBECCA: Yeah

STEVE: You can't save her on your own, Bec

REBECCA: But I understand her

STEVE: Understanding her doesn't mean you know how to help her

REBECCA: But maybe I can

STEVE: Not without proper training. (*Beat*) You need to be careful

REBECCA nods

Report your worries, then leave her alone. Let someone else take the risks. Please. I promised your Mum I'd look after you. (*Beat*) Four weeks

REBECCA smiles, nods, cuddles into him

51

SCENE 4

Same day. 9.30pm. The wasteland. KAY sits at the entrance to the pipe, she holds her legs tight to her body. She wears the same clothes as the previous scene. Blood has dried around the top of her legs. ZOE has just arrived, she carries a sleeping bag, has pulled a parker over the top of thin, scruffy pyjamas and wears beaten-up imitation Ugg boots. KAY doesn't move

ZOE: You alright?

KAY doesn't respond

               What happened?

KAY says nothing. ZOE covers KAY with the sleeping bag. Pause

               Do you want me to go?

KAY: Tell me about Jack Harvey

ZOE: What?

KAY: Did you see him tonight?

ZOE: No

KAY: Pretend you did

ZOE: I don't know what to say

KAY: Tell me about last time

ZOE: OK (*She thinks*) We met outside school

KAY: When it was dark

ZOE: Yeah, it was gone ten. He climbed over the gate with me over his shoulder in a fireman's lift

KAY: (*smiling*) Strong

ZOE: (*playfully*) Bitch. Then we ran to the door of C block and he used his key to get in

KAY: What about the alarm?

ZOE: He flipped open the box just inside the door and punched in the code

KAY: Like James Bond

ZOE: Yeah, just like James Bond

KAY: And you went to the staff room

ZOE: On the top floor. And when we got there he took my hand (*she takes KAY's hand*) and led me to the comfy chairs then he span me around so I was sitting and sat on top of me (*she climbs on top of KAY*) Then he leant in (*she leans over*) and I could smell

KAY: Bleach

ZOE giggles

ZOE: Yeah, domestos

KAY giggles

KAY: Did it turn you on?

53

ZOE:	Yeah. I got all hot and my skin starting tingling
KAY:	That will've been the bleach
ZOE:	(*giggling*) No!
KAY:	And could you feel him?
ZOE:	Yeah
KAY:	But he didn't do anything
ZOE:	He kissed my eyelids (*she kisses KAY's eyelids*) my neck (*she kisses KAY's neck*)
KAY:	(*sits up*) Then

ZOE nods. They kiss. KAY begins to bite

ZOE:	Ow, not like that
KAY:	Sorry
ZOE:	(*with understanding*) It's okay

Beat

KAY:	Did he have a long smooth one?
ZOE:	I don't know yet
KAY:	Because he didn'ae try?
ZOE:	He asked me and I said no
KAY:	And he didn'ae mind?

ZOE shakes her head

ZOE: Said he can wait as long as I need

Beat. KAY nods. Uncouples herself from ZOE

KAY: Do you think you'll marry him

ZOE: Nah. Won't be here much longer

KAY looks up

                  I'll be in the Isle of Muck wi' you

KAY smiles. Beat

                  I'm only practising on him (*beat*) I love you

KAY looks up

KAY: D'you mean it?

ZOE: Wouldn't say it if I didn't

KAY: I need the pill

ZOE: We can go tomorrow

KAY: And some cream

ZOE nods

ZOE: We'll sort it

KAY: Stay wi' me 'til I fall asleep?

ZOE: Course I will

KAY puts her head in ZOE's lap, ZOE strokes her hair

SCENE 5

7.30am the following morning. HAZEL, in the same clothes as the previous scene tidies the flat. Music plays. She is hindered by pain in her ribs. Sporadically she looks at the time. KAY enters. HAZEL stops cleaning

KAY: Wha's all this?

HAZEL: I couldn'ae sleep

KAY: You'll wake Lily

HAZEL: She's gone

KAY: It's seven thirty

HAZEL: Her Da' came early, wanted her back for school

KAY: Well you'll wake the neighbours

HAZEL: (*adjusts the volume*) You didn'ae come home last night

KAY: Didn'ae feel like it

HAZEL winces

             Wha's wrong?

HAZEL: Just a knock (*Beat*) Where've you been?

KAY: What does it matter?

HAZEL: Sit down, I'll make you a breakfast

KAY: Why?

HAZEL: You deserve a treat

KAY: I need a shower

HAZEL: Sit for a minute, eh?

KAY: I've not got long

HAZEL: Got you some smarties for afters. What you
always used to choose

KAY: Aye

HAZEL: Used to pretend each colour did something
different to you

KAY: Like yours

Beat

HAZEL: Eggs and bacon?

KAY: Toast's fine, I can do it maself

HAZEL: Let me

KAY: It makes no difference

KAY makes to leave

HAZEL: Did you spend the night wi' her?

KAY: Who?

HAZEL: Your friend. (*HAZEL produces a photograph
of ZOE and KAY from her pocket*)

KAY: How did you get that?

HAZEL:	Fell out of your pocket. She's prettier now she's older
KAY:	Aye, she is
HAZEL:	Are you dykes now?
KAY:	S'what we've always been
HAZEL:	Have you been getting your fingers wet wi' her?
KAY:	Fuck you
HAZEL:	Please Kay, I'm no' judging. Please. There's nothing in the Isle of Muck, you know
KAY:	–
HAZEL:	S'what it says on the back
KAY:	Give it

KAY rips it from HAZEL's fingers, the action causes a jolt to HAZEL's ribs and she winces

	Wha's goin' on under there?
HAZEL:	S'nothing
KAY:	Show me
HAZEL:	No
KAY:	I said let me look

HAZEL stands still and allows KAY to inspect the bruising on her ribs

	Fucking hell. Who did this?
HAZEL:	Someone got carried away
KAY:	Sit down
HAZEL:	I wanted this morning to be nice
KAY:	Have you had paracetamol?
HAZEL:	I've had stronger than that
KAY:	Right
HAZEL:	He'll not be coming round again
KAY:	You said that last time
HAZEL:	Don't be angry

Beat. KAY looks at the bruising

	Are you leaving me?
KAY:	What if I am?
HAZEL:	Please don't
KAY:	You gave me away
HAZEL:	That was a long time ago
KAY:	So? What difference does that make?
HAZEL:	I had ma' reasons
KAY:	Course you did
HAZEL:	I came back for you though

KAY:	Aye, when it suited you. I cried for hours. Nan was going crazy cos I wouldn'ae stop asking her why, what I'd done wrong but she couldn'ae tell me. I kept imagining you all at home without me, glad I was gone. Then after a few days I decided it must be because you just didn't like me. And Nan was so kind that I started to like it – made maself forget – and then a couple of months later you came back, rowed wi' Nan in the kitchen and put me in the car. You were so angry I didn't dare speak. When we got home everyone was gone – Dave, and the little ones gone, just like that and you didn'ae say a thing just went to bed and left me on ma own
HAZEL:	You've no idea
KAY:	Why did you send me away?
HAZEL:	You don't remember what it was like, so many of us, on top of each other
KAY:	And I was the one that didn'ae fit
HAZEL:	It was hard
KAY:	Get me out of the way and you could be a proper family
HAZEL:	No
KAY:	But they left anyway, so you came back for me
HAZEL:	You were mine

60

KAY: But you've never liked me

HAZEL: I don't have to, I'm your mother

The doorbell rings

KAY: I'll go

HAZEL: Kay. I try ma' best

KAY re-enters with ZOE who stands in just her knickers, school shirt and shoes

KAY: Wait here

ZOE and HAZEL are left alone. ZOE is desperately embarrassed

HAZEL: What happened to your trousers?

ZOE: Someone took them

HAZEL: Mini mouse. Nice

ZOE: They're old ones.

HAZEL: You've got bigger

ZOE nods, mortified

                She told me what you are

ZOE looks at her confused

                What you do to each other?

ZOE: I –

HAZEL: You be careful of ma daughter

HAZEL lets her gown fall open so that ZOE can see the bruising.
KAY comes back and HAZEL quickly replaces it. KAY throws
a pair of leggings to ZOE

KAY: S'all I've got

ZOE: S'fine

ZOE scrabbles to get them on as they are too small

KAY: See you later

HAZEL: Don't forget your smarties

KAY: You eat them

KAY and ZOE exit

SCENE 6

4.30pm the same day. Down by the river. A tyre hangs from a rope to make a swing. KAY sits on it, cigarette in hand. ZOE enters.

ZOE: Fucking hell Kayleigh Grey

KAY looks up with a jolt, then realises it is ZOE

                       Her head was on fire

KAY: Are the police still there?

ZOE: Aye. They're still taking statements

KAY: Did you give yours?

ZOE: I lied. But everyone knows

KAY: Told you I'd make her pay for it

ZOE smiles, unsure

ZOE: She must've been wearing loads of hairspray – her whole hair just went up. They're saying she'll have first degree burns on her scalp

KAY: Did you see her face? Eyeballs nearly popped out of her head

ZOE laughs nervously

ZOE: You really don't give a fuck

KAY: I wasn't gonnae let her get away with it – twice in one day

ZOE: I wouldn'ae have the guts

KAY:	That's what I'm here for
ZOE:	You're in so much trouble
KAY:	Worth it though
ZOE:	Not if they lock you up
KAY:	Tha' won't. It was an accident (*she smirks*)
ZOE:	S'that what you told the police?
KAY:	Aye
ZOE:	She's gonnae look like a boy
KAY:	(*pleased*) I know, from now on she's Duncan Mc-Tit-Face
ZOE:	We'll never be allowed to use Bunsen burners again
KAY:	I know. They'll make a law against it
ZOE:	Grey's Law
KAY:	(*laughs*) I'll go down in the history books
ZOE:	Maybe you shouldn'ae do these things Kay?
KAY:	I was right behind her. I couldn'ae miss the opportunity
ZOE:	No / but
KAY:	/ And where were you? Eh? Cowering behind the science benches in ski-pants from lost property. Your fucking moose-knuckle on show

ZOE:	I don't want trouble Kay
KAY:	She can't just make a twat of you
ZOE:	I don't care
KAY:	Well I do
ZOE:	I was frightened
KAY:	Oh for fuck sake. She's a coward
ZOE:	No. I was frightened of you
KAY:	Me? Of me? I love you, you daft bint
ZOE:	Aye. But you go wild
KAY:	I thought you liked that?
ZOE:	Kay stop it, I'm serious
KAY:	So am I. She took your dignity
ZOE:	It's OK, I can put up with it
KAY:	No, why should you?
ZOE:	I... You just went too far
KAY:	Fuck off. Don't I get a thank you?
ZOE:	Everyone knows you hate her
KAY:	So?
ZOE:	And you were standing right there

KAY:	Doesn'ae mean a thing. And no-one actually saw – 'cept you. We were right at the back of the classroom
ZOE:	They all think you did it on purpose. They're saying all kinds of things about us
KAY:	You worried about what Jack Harvey's gonna think?
ZOE:	I just don't want to draw attention Kay
KAY:	But we're savages
ZOE:	Not yet we're not
KAY:	In our souls
ZOE:	(*taking her hand*) I'm just scared, that they're gonn'ae take you away
KAY:	With nae evidence there's nothing tha' can do. Miss Hastie'll stick up for me
ZOE:	Mibee
KAY:	Who needs her anyway, when we're in the Isle of Muck? Bet she can't even ride a horse

She looks at ZOE

	What?
ZOE:	She always helps you. She's so nice
KAY:	Why would I need her when I've got you?

ZOE smiles weakly. Silence

ZOE: There's gonna be loads a questions

KAY: I've got loads of answers

ZOE laughs

ZOE: Ma' Mum says you've got a silver tongue

KAY: Want to find out? (*she waggles it provocatively*)

ZOE smiles, nervous. KAY grabs her so ZOE is sitting on the swing with her

                Remember the day we met?

ZOE: Aye

KAY: You were crying cos you'd lost your doll in the river an' I told you to follow me cos I'd just found this (*she indicates the swing they sit on*)

ZOE: It was covered in oil but you didn'ae give a shit, just jumped on, got grease all over you

KAY laughs

KAY: An' you stood laughing, telling me the trouble I'd be in

ZOE: Aye

KAY: I knew you wanted a go though

ZOE: So you said, "I've an idea" and you're your clothes right off and went on it in your pants. Said we could jump in the river after and no-one would ever know

KAY: Just wanted you to get naked

ZOE: I had a feeling in ma tummy, like a tickle, I knew I shouldn'ae but I couldn't resist

KAY: I didn'ae think you would

ZOE: Nor did I

KAY: You were taking your clothes off saying you shouldn't be taking your clothes off but you had this grin on your face

ZOE: I'd never met anyone like you

KAY: And you weren't wearing a bra but you had these tiny little breasts

ZOE: Stop it

KAY starts to swing

KAY: When I got home ma Ma went spare but I told her I'd been attacked by some older girls

ZOE: And she believed you?

KAY: No (*beat*) But she couldn'ae prove otherwise so she couldn'ae beat me

ZOE smiles

          The thing about truth is, that as long as there are no witnesses, it doesn'ae have to be true

ZOE tries to wrap her head around this, fails, laughs

ZOE: I found that doll on the way home (*beat*)
Never played wi' her again

KAY: Ten was too old for that shit

Beat

ZOE: You must be freezing

KAY: Nah. Got Irn-Bru running through ma veins

ZOE smiles

ZOE: D'you ever hit her back?

KAY is silent

'Cos, for what it's worth, I wouldn'ae blame
you. If you did

Beat

KAY: I'm fucking starving

ZOE: (*delving in her bag*) I've got space raiders

She throws the crisps to KAY. KAY eats.

Wish you could come back to mine but my
Ma / m

KAY: / Doesn'ae ma / tter

ZOE: / Once she's made her mind up

KAY: Yeah

ZOE: And if she hears

KAY kisses her

> They're gonna put you away Kay, I know it.
> Then what'll I do?

Beat. KAY moves to her

KAY: Twenty-second hour on the twenty second
day twenty-twenty-two, I'll meet you here

ZOE: (*laughs*) Are you serious?

KAY: Why not?

ZOE: That's years away

KAY: Worst case scenario

ZOE: We'll be (*works it out*) twenty ni–...

KAY: Thirty. So if we get separated we'll always
know, just to hold on

ZOE nods. KAY winks, exits

SCENE 7

An hour later. HAZEL's flat. HAZEL crosses herself in front of a picture of Christ that hangs on the wall, she recites the Lord's prayer. A bowl, kettle and towel lay on the coffee table. KAY enters

KAY: What's goin on?

HAZEL: Whoever causes one of these little ones who believe in me to sin, it would be better for him if a great millstone were hung around his neck and he were thrown into the sea

KAY: What you on about?

HAZEL: You've ruined me, like I always knew you would

KAY: It was an accident

HAZEL: A false witness shall be punished and a liar shall be caught

KAY: It was only her hair

HAZEL: God forgive me

KAY: She deserved it

HAZEL: Sit

HAZEL indicates the coffee table, KAY turns to run, HAZEL blocks her escape

KAY: No

HAZEL: I SAID SIT

71

KAY sits in front of the table, this is a ritual she recognises

> Hand

KAY holds her right hand over the bowl

HAZEL: Left

Obediently KAY replaces her right hand for her left

HAZEL: Say it

KAY: Wash me thoroughly from my iniquity, and cleanse me from my sin

HAZEL: Please

KAY: Please

HAZEL nods, stuffs a rag of material into KAY's mouth, then pours boiling water from the kettle over her left hand. KAY writhes in pain

HAZEL: Bear it

KAY struggles to contain her screams

> He that covers his sins shall not prosper: but whoever confesses and forsakes them shall have mercy. Repent you therefore, and be converted, that your sins may be blotted out. If we confess our sins, he is faithful and just and will forgive us our sins and purify us from all unrighteousness. (*Beat*) What do you say?

KAY: Thank-you

HAZEL: To him

KAY stands in front of the picture of Christ

KAY: Thank you

HAZEL: Take off your trousers

KAY: Enough now

HAZEL: I'll say when it's enough

KAY does as she is instructed

              Knickers

KAY: (*defiant*) No

HAZEL: Do it

KAY starts to remove her knickers. In the distance a police siren is heard, HAZEL is startled. It grows in volume throughout the following

              Get them back on. They're coming for you

KAY: Who?

HAZEL: Police. Social services. I told them you're too much

KAY: Tha'll take me away, then what will you do?

HAZEL: You'll be back. And I'll no' be blamed for your crimes

A police siren becomes loud, then ceases. The doorbell rings

You have sinned against the Lord, be sure your sin will find you out. (*Beat*) And just so you know, I've warned them you're a fantasist. (*She looks at her hand*) Nasty accident making your tea

SCENE 8

*Six weeks later. End of May. A park. STEVE and REBECCA
sit with baby ROSIE – 5 and a half weeks old – in a pram*

REBECCA: Has she gone?

STEVE: Yeah, dead to the world

REBECCA smiles, closes her eyes

REBECCA: You've got the knack

STEVE: I don't know about that. It's probably just
the paint fumes

REBECCA laughs

REBECCA: Shall we find another sand dune?

STEVE: You mean...?

REBECCA: (*shrugs playfully*) Why not? We always said
two

STEVE: Do we need a sand dune?

*They laugh and kiss. ZOE enters, she carries a doll and a felt tip
pen, she watches awkwardly*

REBECCA: We should probably wait a few months

He nods, strokes her hair behind her ear

STEVE: After the instillation?

REBECCA: Yeah

ZOE: (*finding the courage to interrupt*) Miss

REBECCA: (*turning*) Zoe, I wasn't expect / ing

ZOE: / It's born

REBECCA: She

ZOE: A girl! Can I have a look?

REBECCA: Er, yes

STEVE: (*protective*) Quiet though, she's just gone off

ZOE: What's her name?

REBECCA: Rosie

ZOE quietly approaches the pram and peeps in

ZOE: Och, she's beautiful

REBECCA smiles

(*to STEVE*) She looks like you

STEVE smiles awkwardly

How many weeks is she?

REBECCA: Five… and a half

ZOE: She's so wee

REBECCA: She was premature

ZOE: How much did she weigh?

REBECCA: Four pounds thirteen

ZOE: Oh, that's so tiny

STEVE:	(*warning*) Becca
REBECCA:	Well, we should be –
ZOE:	Kay'll be back in a few weeks

REBECCA glances at STEVE

REBECCA:	How is she?
ZOE:	I don't know, we're not allowed to speak
REBECCA:	Right
ZOE:	But I asked at school and they told me it was only an eight week placement so…
STEVE:	(*firmly*) Becca
ZOE:	I bet she'll love meeting her when she gets home
STEVE:	Time to go
REBECCA:	Yes. Well, it's been lovely to see you Zoe
ZOE:	Aye, and you Miss
REBECCA:	You take care now

REBECCA and STEVE exit. ZOE sits down and takes out pen, thinks. Moments later, STEVE returns, grabs ZOE by the wrist. She scrabbles to her feet

STEVE:	You stay right away
ZOE:	Sorry?
STEVE:	You and your friend

ZOE: I'll not come –

STEVE: Or I'll not be responsible for my actions

ZOE is stunned. STEVE lets go his grip and she runs away. He stands, breathes heavily. REBECCA returns

REBECCA: Did you find it?

STEVE: No. Must've left it at home. Let's go

REBECCA and STEVE exit.

SCENE 9

Three and a half weeks later. 4.30pm. The wasteland. ZOE and KAY look at each other

ZOE: Hey

KAY: Wondered when you'd get here

ZOE: Tha' took ma phone so I couldn'ae text and tha' wouldn'ae let me write

KAY: Doesn'ae matter now. (*Beat*) So you've no' forgotten me?

ZOE: (*slightly sheepish*) Course no'. (*Beat*) I heard you were back

KAY: You heard right

ZOE: I'm no's'posed to see you

KAY: No change there then. Come here

They kiss

ZOE: What were they like?

KAY: People trying too hard to be nice

Beat

ZOE: You look… fatter

KAY: Cheeky bitch

ZOE: Suits you

KAY: Well if you like it

KAY smiles, ZOE tries

ZOE: Why'd they make you go?

KAY: Said ma' Mum needed a rest from me. That I was making her ill

ZOE: 'Cos of what happened with Donna?

KAY: That was just the icing on the cake. S'what the social worker said

ZOE: Will you have to go to court?

KAY: Probably not. I said it was an accident, she said it was on purpose so it's my word against hers and no witnesses

KAY looks at ZOE. ZOE smiles

ZOE: Do they think you're mad?

KAY: Why d'you say that? Who said that?

ZOE: (*shrugs*) People

KAY: S'that what you think?

ZOE: No

Beat

KAY: Tha' said I'm crazy

ZOE: Really?

KAY: No

ZOE: Did they ask a lot of questions?

KAY:	Aye. Bit like you.
ZOE:	But you're home now?
KAY:	Aye
ZOE:	For good?
KAY:	Aye
ZOE:	I wish you hadn'ae gone away
KAY:	(*smiles*) It was only eight weeks

She pulls ZOE to her, it is a little awkward

> What's the matter?

ZOE:	Nothing. (*changing the subject*) How's your Ma?
KAY:	On a lot of pills

ZOE nods KAY flicks a lighter. Moments pass

ZOE:	I bought you a present
KAY:	Is it chocolate?
ZOE:	No! I wanted to send it to you but they wouldn'ae let me. Said it was childish

She pulls out her doll

> But it wasn'ae. It was the only way I could think to send you ma' new number

KAY smiles, undresses the doll to reveal the telephone number written on the doll's body

81

	(*laughing*) I knew you'd take her clothes off. Impressed?
KAY:	Very
ZOE:	Have it now

Beat

	Are you back at school?
KAY:	Three days a week
ZOE:	And?
KAY:	Different building same shite
ZOE:	Mam says you were expelled
KAY:	No. 'Advised to move on'. (*Beat*) Tell me something nice Zo, are they leaving you alone?
ZOE:	Aye, you did good.
KAY:	(*smiles*) Well tha's alright then
ZOE:	Donna came back last week but she won't look at anyone. She has to wear a wig. Someone pulled it off in maths and everyone screamed 'cos her scalp is purple and her hair is in these weird tufts

KAY smiles. ZOE searches for something else to say

	Miss Hastie had her baby. They announced it in assembly. She's called Rosie. She came early and she's ever so pretty

KAY: You saw her?

ZOE: Aye, just once when she was pushing her in the pram

A silence falls

KAY: (*turning to ZOE*) Will you do it with me?

ZOE: Do what?

KAY: Isle of Muck?

Beat. ZOE shakes her head

Hey? It'll be a new life, just you and me

ZOE: I've fucked everything up

KAY: What you talking about?

ZOE: I didn'ae realise

KAY: What?

ZOE: Jack Harvey. I let him touch me

KAY: You mean?

ZOE: I didn'ae know it could happen when you were on your period, I thought

KAY: You're pregnant?

ZOE: (*nods*) I wasn'ae cheating, I was lonely, I was just foolin' around while I was waitin'

KAY: No, no, no. Don't you tell me that

ZOE: I just wanted to do it, to feel normal

KAY: (*explodes*) NO (*pushes her*) NO (*pushes her again*) NO (*pushes her again*) NO

ZOE: It's you I love

ZOE covers her face with her hands

KAY: Does he know?

ZOE: No

KAY: So get rid of it. It's easy. I'll come wi' you

ZOE: Ma' Mam won't let me, she says I'd go to hell

KAY: You told your Ma?

ZOE: I was scared Kay

KAY: What if he raped you?

ZOE: What?

KAY: What if it was rape?

ZOE: It wasn't. I wanted it

KAY: No-one else knows that. He's older than you

ZOE: So?

KAY: So you could say he forced you

ZOE: But he didn't

KAY: Don't you get it, you can say what you like

ZOE: I don't want to Kay, he'd get into trouble

KAY: Why are you so fuckin' weak?

KAY goes to punch her but stops herself

                   How could you do this?

ZOE: I'm so sorry

KAY: Fuck off Zoe

ZOE exits. KAY regains her composure. She sits, picks up the doll, tears off its arms and legs.

SCENE 10

Later the same day, 6pm. The wasteland. Baby gurgles come from within one of the concrete pipes. ZOE enters

ZOE: Kay? Kay are y'here?

KAY: (*from within a pipe*) Aye

ZOE: I wasn'ae expecting you to text

KAY: Someone I'd like you to meet

ZOE: What you talking about?

KAY emerges from the pipe holding baby ROSIE, 9 weeks old

                 Christ Almighty what have you done...?

KAY: You'll never guess who this is

ZOE: I...?

KAY: Don't you recognise her? This is Rosie

ZOE: Miss. Hastie's Rosie?

KAY: Aye. Thought I'd show her the pipes. Do you want a hold? Get some practise in?

ZOE: No. Fuckin hell Kay. What've you got her for?

KAY: Only borrowing her. Thought we could have some fun

ZOE: Does Miss Hastie know you've got her?

KAY: What do you think?

86

ZOE: I'm no' being part of this

KAY: She'd left her in the garden in her carry cot

ZOE: You went to her house

KAY: Why not?

ZOE: This is fucked up

KAY: I climbed over the fence. Like Lara Croft

ZOE: She'll be goin' out of her mind

KAY: Calm down. Look. (*she shows ZOE the baby*) What do you think? Look at her little body. Hold her, go on

ZOE: I don't want to

KAY: She's so tiny. We can bring yours down here when it's born

ZOE: What have you taken?

KAY: This 'n that, what's it matter?

ZOE: She's crying Kay, she wants her Mam. Please

KAY: She's hungry aren't you. Look what I've got

KAY pulls out some chocolate buttons

ZOE: She cann'ae eat yet. Look, she's no' got any teeth

KAY: Alright then

KAY reaches into her bag and brings out a bottle of Irn-Bru

ZOE:	No
KAY:	She'll love it, it's Irn-Bru, what's not to like?
ZOE:	(*starting to cry*) Please Kay, you can't give that to a baby. She needs Miss. Hastie's tit
KAY:	Who doesn'ae?

KAY pours the drink into ROSIE's mouth

> Look she loves it

ZOE is panicking

> Bet it's the tastiest thing she's ever had

ROSIE starts to choke

> Think it went down the wrong hole. We need to wind her (*she starts to hit her back a little too roughly*) see, I'm good wi' babies

ZOE:	Let's just take her back now Kay? Before she wees or shits or something
KAY:	No, she just needs a little sleep
ZOE:	We could just leave her there. Make an anonymous phone call. Then you wouln'ae get into any trouble

KAY takes the baby into the pipe. The screaming continues

KAY:	(*from inside the pipe*) Look how dark it is Rosie, like being back in mummy's tummy

Sound of a police car

ZOE:	Come on Kay, I can hear a police car.
	(*yelling*) Over here

KAY reappears from the tunnel with ROSIE who continues to cry

KAY:	What you doin?

ZOE:	Over here

KAY:	I've got it all figured out. We'll get a flat, when it's born. You and me

ZOE:	No

KAY:	Why not?

ZOE:	Give her to me

KAY:	You're not listening

ZOE:	You're scaring her

KAY:	Why can't we be together?

ZOE:	We just can't

KAY:	You said you loved me

ZOE:	I do, more than anyone

KAY:	So prove it

ZOE:	I can't

KAY:	You don't have to stay wi' Jack

ZOE:	Please Kay, we can talk about this later

KAY:	No now
ZOE:	No
KAY:	Now
ZOE:	No
KAY:	Why not? (*KAY holds the baby up, threatening to drop her*) WHY NOT?
ZOE:	I'M MARRYING JACK

KAY explodes, starts to hyperventilate

> Give her to me, Kayleigh. Kayleigh, give her to me

They struggle. To get ROSIE away from ZOE, KAY dives into the pipe. ROSIE continues to cry. Suddenly the screaming comes to an abrupt end. KAY comes out of the pipe. ZOE and KAY look at each other. ZOE runs away. KAY looks back into the pipe. The police siren gets louder.

Lights fade.

Interval

ACT 2 SCENE 1

*2019. January. 12am. Brighton. The seafront. KAY, 27, and
JOHN, 32, are drinking Stella from cans.*

JOHN: Three, two, one

*Fireworks go off. Cheering in the distance. They kiss, look out to
sea*

              So what now?

KAY: Drink and enjoy the view

He laughs, looks at her

              Stop gawping at us

JOHN laughs, KAY smiles

JOHN: You're beautiful

KAY: Oh no, you can stop that

JOHN: I'm doing romance

KAY: Well let me tell you now John Parker, I'm
              no' getting sand up my bottom for you

He laughs

JOHN: New year's resolution?

KAY: Fuck that

JOHN: Come on – one thing for twenty-nineteen

KAY: No

JOHN:	Tell me something then
KAY:	What?
JOHN:	Something I don't know
KAY:	V-E+F = 2
JOHN:	(*laughs*) Euler's equation. Knew that
KAY:	Might've bloody known
JOHN:	I meant something about /you
KAY:	/ I know what you meant. I'm no' playin'
JOHN:	Come on Trace, this is what lovers do
KAY:	Oh, is that what we are?
JOHN:	It's been ten months
KAY:	Has it?
JOHN:	Go on Trace, humour me
KAY:	No. Ma favourite colour's green
JOHN:	Knew that too. Something else.
KAY:	Like what?
JOHN:	Where did you go to school?
KAY:	Scotland
JOHN:	Oh right, that's a great insight

She smirks

	Who was your favourite teacher?
KAY:	No
JOHN:	Why do you never talk about your childhood?
KAY:	Stop
JOHN:	Trace
KAY:	I've said no
JOHN:	Three facts, which one's true, go on
KAY:	Leave it
JOHN:	Alright, I'll go first. One: when I was fourteen I had an asthma attack on a school trip to Ben Nevis and had to be rescued by an air ambulance because I'd forgotten my inhaler, two: I lost my virginity to a girl I'd never met at a party when I was nineteen or, three: I was the youngest person in England to achieve the gold Duke of Edinburgh award
KAY:	The asthma attack
JOHN:	(*disappointed*) Bollocks. I'd thought you'd go for the award

KAY smirks

	I don't even use my inhaler anymore
KAY:	You wheeze when you come

JOHN:	Cheeky devil

He wrestles her for a kiss

	Right, your turn
KAY:	Still no
JOHN:	Fair's fair
KAY:	I'd like to have a dog one day
JOHN:	What about children?

KAY freezes

KAY:	Dunno
JOHN:	I would
KAY:	Right
JOHN:	With you
KAY:	John stop it, we're not there yet
JOHN:	(*pulling out a box and opening it to reveal a ring*) Are we here?
KAY:	No, God no, fucking hell John
JOHN:	So where are we?
KAY:	We're having fun
JOHN:	And that's it?
KAY:	Yeah
JOHN:	I'm just a shag?

KAY: No

JOHN: So what?

KAY: I don't know. It is what it is

JOHN: How can we move forward if you won't let
            me / get close

KAY: / Why do we have to move forward?

JOHN: It's how relationships work

KAY: Then I'm not

JOHN: W / hat?

KAY: / Cut out for relationships

JOHN: Is it me? Do you not fancy me?

KAY: Course I fancy you

JOHN: And you like being with me?

KAY: Yes

JOHN: So what's the problem? I thought this was
            going somewhere

KAY: Did you?

JOHN: I thought you did too

KAY: I like being with you, it's fun

JOHN: Fun?! And that's enough for you is it? (*Beat*)
            Is it? Cos I'm falling for you Tracey. I *have*
            fallen for you

She is silent

> But if you're telling me it's never going to
> happen, that I'm just a bit of fun, then I'll
> walk away

Silence

> Right, right

JOHN gets up to go

KAY: It can never be more

JOHN: Is there someone else?

KAY: No

JOHN: Am I not good enough?

KAY: No

JOHN: So what? If you're gonna break my fucking
               heart at least tell me why

KAY: I thought I could do this but I can't. It's no'
               fair

JOHN: On who?

KAY: You. I've tried before and it doesn'ae work

JOHN: You're too young to think like that

KAY: Don't tell me what I am

JOHN: I'm not... I'm just... everyone gets hurt

KAY: It's not that

JOHN:	Then what? I don't – (*suddenly tender*) Did something happen to you? Tracey, did some / one
KAY:	/ Stop
JOHN:	Just talk to me
KAY:	I don't want to, I don't want to spoil it

They look at each other, they have reached a hiatus

	I'm no' the person you think I am
JOHN:	What do you mean?
KAY:	Threefacts, which one's true. One: I was expelled from two schools before I was fifteen, two: when I was fourteen I set a girl's hair on fire and gave her first degree burns on her scalp, three: when I was twelve I deliberately broke ma' mother's arm in two places (*Beat*) All of them. I can't be what you want me to be. I'd love to share memories that would make you blush and giggle and love me more but I can't because my memories would turn your stomach inside out
JOHN:	What?
KAY:	I did something
JOHN:	--

KAY:	And I can never make it right. If I could undo it, if I could get out of this skin (*she scratches violently at her body*) but it's no good.
JOHN:	Tracey
KAY:	Tracey doesn'ae exist
JOHN:	You're not ma / king
KAY:	/ Walk away John
JOHN:	I won't. Whatever it is –
KAY:	I'm telling you
JOHN:	And I'm telling you, I'll love you whatever you've done. Nothing will change that
KAY:	Except this. (*Beat*) I'm Kayleigh Grey

He is still

So go on. It's ruined now

He stands motionless, stunned

You do know what that means don't you?

He stares at her. Silence

You're right, there are no words. So now you understand? That I was doing you a favour.

JOHN:	You were that girl
KAY:	Aye. I wish I wasn'ae but I was

JOHN looks at her

	(*thumps her chest*) Go on, hurt me. Go on, do it for her
JOHN:	(*recovering himself, breathless*) You can't be
KAY:	But I am, I'm so sorry. It'll be easier now cos you can hate me (*beat*) I'll no' see you again

KAY leaves, JOHN watches her go then calls out

JOHN:	I don't hate you
KAY:	(*spins*) What?
JOHN:	I don't hate you, I never expected... but I don't hate you
KAY:	Why not? What the fuck's wrong with you?
JOHN:	Stay
KAY:	Did you no' read the papers? What I did?

JOHN nods

	What these hands have done? Are you no' afraid?
JOHN:	Should I be? I want to get to know you
KAY:	Why?
JOHN:	Because I like you
KAY:	You like Tracey
JOHN:	I like the person I met in Stacey's Rock Bar, who gets excited when they play 'Stairway

to Heaven', who gets drunk on one can of
Stella.

KAY is silent

That's not Tracey that's you

KAY: You won't like the rest of it

JOHN: Maybe

KAY: (*suddenly*) Fuck me, are you a reporter?

JOHN: No

KAY: Are you writing a book?

JOHN: (*shakes his head*) You know who I am. Trace,
look at me. I want to get to know you. You.
This person standing in front of me right
now. One wish what would it be?

KAY: Not to have done what I did

JOHN: Can't have that, it's impossible

KAY: (*thinks*) To live a normal life (*beat*) To work,
to have a family, to have roots. And for
someone to know me

JOHN nods

I need to tell you everything. All of it. And
when I have, it'll be your choice, stay or
walk away

JOHN: Okay

SCENE 2

2019. April. Early evening. Cemetery in Scotstoun. REBECCA now 46, stands beside ROSIE's grave. STEVE, 47, enters with a crutch. A small acknowledgment passes between them. Neither says anything for some time

STEVE: You brought tulips

REBECCA: They flowered just in time

He smiles

STEVE: Which colour won the race this year?

REBECCA: Orange

STEVE: Ah, I had my money on purple

They smile

They're beautiful

REBECCA: (*nods, looks at him*) You look… good. Strong.

STEVE: I've been going to the gym

REBECCA: Suits you

STEVE: You think?

REBECCA: Always did

Beat

STEVE: You're look / ing

REBECCA: (*deliberately cutting him off*) / Did you bring the cake?

101

STEVE: Yes

He rustles in his bag and brings out a tin which he opens to reveal a beautifully decorated cake with a number 13 candle

REBECCA: It's exquisite

He smiles

STEVE: It had to be special this year. Turning into a teen –

REBECCA: I get it

STEVE: That's why I just went for one candle, more discreet

REBECCA: You made it?

STEVE: Of course

REBECCA: Not –

STEVE: I made it, Bec. Just me

She nods

                   Are you ready?

REBECCA: Yeah

Carefully he takes out a lighter and lights the candles, his hand is shaking

                   I don't think I can sing

STEVE: We'll just blow the candles

He finishes lighting and they watch them flicker for a few moments.

(*gently*) Ready?

REBECCA nods, then together they blow out the candles

Silence

(*indicating the cake*) Would you like –

REBECCA shakes her head

I'll take it for –

REBECCA: Thirteen. Do you imagine her…?

STEVE nods

I do it all the time. What she would look like. What she would *be* like. Would she still look like you? Or would my genes have taken over. (*Beat*) I wonder if she would have liked me. If we would have been friends as well. I like imagining that, the things we would have done together

She stops, realises she has spoken a lot

Sorry. Sorry

STEVE: Don't be

She composes herself

REBECCA: How are Cassie and the girls?

STEVE: Becca

REBECCA:	What?
STEVE:	Let's not. This is. This is Rosie's day
REBECCA:	She just gets one day, does she?
STEVE:	That's not what I meant
REBECCA:	Sorry. (*Beat*) True though. Not a bad thing. You compartmentalise. Always did. Put things in boxes in your head while you did something else
STEVE:	Don't tell me what I do

They are silent

	I did my best
REBECCA:	Did you?
STEVE:	I said we could try again
REBECCA:	Replace her?
STEVE:	No
REBECCA:	Two months later?
STEVE:	I
REBECCA:	I could still feel the sensation of her
STEVE:	I didn't come here for this
REBECCA:	Sorry, I'm sorry I'm sorry Steve

STEVE nods

It's just, it's just this... all the time. This, this... loss. People say it doesn't get better you just get better at it (*beat*) But I haven't. Nearly thirteen years and I'm still... (*she looks at him*) I think it must be people like you that they're talking about

STEVE: How can you say that when I'm stood here like this?

REBECCA: But since then

STEVE: Is that what you think?

REBECCA: It's what I see

STEVE: Because I'm trying to have a life

REBECCA: Yes

STEVE: You think that means she meant less to me?

REBECCA: That's no / t

STEVE: / You think she's not in my mind every single day?

REBECCA: I didn't say that

STEVE: Then what?

REBECCA: You moved on

STEVE: From you

REBECCA is winded

I didn't mean that

REBECCA: Yes you did

STEVE: I couldn't bear to see you in that much pain.

REBECCA: So you left

STEVE: Is that why you're so angry?

REBECCA: I'm angry because you survived and I don't know how... and yes... because you left me

STEVE: I didn't know that was what I was doing

REBECCA: Really?

STEVE: I'd always planned to come back

REBECCA: You've never said that before

STEVE: It was only supposed to be a few weeks, in my head. Get some... clarity

REBECCA: And then you met Cassie

STEVE nods

Did you not think what that would do to me?

STEVE: I was trying not to think. And she made it go away

REBECCA: So I didn't stand a chance

STEVE: It wasn't a competition...

Moments pass

REBECCA: Do you still blame me?

STEVE: No

REBECCA: Why not? I let that girl into our lives. I invited her into our marriage – your words. Because I wanted to save her, thought I knew better than everyone else

STEVE: It wasn't your fault Bec

REBECCA: Wasn't it? You used to think so

STEVE: I should never have said that

REBECCA: Tell me how you did it Steve

STEVE: What?

REBECCA: Built something new

STEVE: (*shrugs*) It just happened

REBECCA: I can't

STEVE: You have

REBECCA: Have I?

She cries. He moves to her but she turns away

STEVE: Cassie thinks you're incredible. Setting up the charity

REBECCA: It's all I can do. So I can talk about her every day. To make her life matter

STEVE nods

                But I'm so tired (*beat*) Of the anger. Of the guilt

STEVE: Never goes away

REBECCA looks at him

        I was her Dad. I had one job. And I failed

They stand in silence

        They brought her here. (*Beat*) Her care workers. The final step in her rehabilitation. To make it real. (*Beat*) Stood her in front of her grave so she could see the place we'd chosen for her. Read our words. (*He shakes his head. Beat*) I tried again

REBECCA: Steve

STEVE: Cassie found me… She was devastated. And kind. And then she told me I had to find a way. To forgive myself

REBECCA: And have you?

He gives her a small smile

STEVE: Come to dinner

REBECCA: No

STEVE: Please. Cassie worries about you

REBECCA: And you?

STEVE: Course I do. But you're stronger than you think

She looks at him

You've touched so many people

REBECCA: Yet the only person that matters walked away

STEVE: I know

REBECCA: Now I'm in one of your boxes

STEVE: That's not true

REBECCA: Do you think we could have made it? If she hadn't died?

STEVE: Bec

REBECCA: But do you think?

STEVE nods

I loved you

STEVE: I know

REBECCA: It wasn't perfect but it was…

STEVE: I know

REBECCA: We were happy, weren't we?

STEVE: (*he nods*) It's gone Bec

REBECCA: Do you have it with Cassie?

STEVE: I love her

REBECCA: But is it the same?

STEVE: I love her and we're good together

REBECCA: But is it the same?

STEVE: (*after a pause*) 'Course it bloody isn't. But it's what I've got. And people need me

REBECCA: But who needs me?

STEVE: I do. I need you.

REBECCA nods. They stand, breathing. STEVE takes her hand

SCENE 3

2019. Late-May – almost five months after Act 2 Scene 1. 11pm.
Brighton – the seafront. KAY, in a wedding dress, dances to
faint music, JOHN watches her

KAY:	We should get back. Our guests'll be thinking the worst
JOHN:	Our guests will be drinking Bollinger – they won't be thinking anything

KAY laughs

	Look at you… Tracey Parker
KAY:	Fuckin' hell I sound like a secretary
JOHN:	I think it sounds beautiful
KAY:	You would
JOHN:	Are you happy?
KAY:	Aye
JOHN:	Are you sure?
KAY:	More than I thought possible

JOHN smiles

	More than I deserve
JOHN:	No
KAY:	Aye
JOHN:	Not today. You promised

KAY nods

JOHN: This is ours. Our day. Yours and mine.
              Tracey and John. New chapter. We start
              from today and we don't look back

She nods. Looks at him with a glint in her eye

              What? What's that look for?

KAY: There's something you should know. About
              the honeymoon

He waits

JOHN: What? Oh no

KAY: There's goin' to be someone joining us

JOHN: (*confused*) Who?

KAY glances down at her belly

              You mean?

KAY: (*she nods*) Putting up with all that sex wasn't
              for nothing

She laughs

JOHN: We're having a baby, WE'RE HAVING A
              BABY

He picks her up and swings her round

KAY: Careful

JOHN: Oh sorry, sorry

He kisses her belly

Hello in there

KAY: I don't think it can hear you yet, it's only the size of an orange seed

JOHN: (*laughs*) How long have you known?

KAY: Coupl'a weeks

JOHN: Couple of weeks? And you didn't say anything?

KAY: I was waiting to be sure, you know, checked by a doctor

JOHN: And we can definitely keep it?

KAY: You know we can, and Sally was delighted

JOHN: (*mock outrage*) You told your bloody parole officer before me?!

KAY: She guessed

JOHN: How?

KAY: I don't know, I must be glowing or something (*beat*) She knew we were trying, since tha' said we could (*giggling*) And she's seen how exhausted I've been

JOHN laughs. It subsides, they look at each other

I'm sorry it can't be straightforward

JOHN: Simplicity's over rated

KAY: They said I'm fit to be a mother

JOHN: I know. You are Trace

KAY: Am I?

JOHN: (*nods*) I wouldn't choose anyone else to do
              this with

KAY: I don't believe that

JOHN: Are you forgetting what day it is? Look at
              yourself

She laughs

              Come here you big bundle of loveliness (*he
              snuffles her belly*)

KAY: What did I do to deserve you?

JOHN: I don't know but you're stuck with me now.
              (*Beat*) This is the beginning Trace

KAY: I'd like chickens too

JOHN: What?

KAY: Some land and some chickens

JOHN: OK

KAY: Be self-sufficient, just you and me and her

JOHN: Her?

KAY: Aye

JOHN: How d'you know that?

KAY:	I can feel it
JOHN:	(*laughs*) Whatever you want
KAY:	Really?
JOHN:	Really

He kisses her

SCENE 4

2020. Late-January – eight months later. Scotstoun. Mid-morning. A park, REBECCA sits on a bench. STEVE arrives

STEVE: You wanted to see me? You could've come to the house. Cassie would've loved / to see

REBECCA: / I saw her. This morning (*beat*) at the petrol station

STEVE: Who?

REBECCA: Her. Kayleigh Grey (*beat*) It was her, Steve

STEVE: Come on Bec, we've been here before

REBECCA: No. This time I'm sure

STEVE: You're always sure

REBECCA: Not like this. I'd put my life on it

STEVE: It's been fourteen years

REBECCA: It wasn't just the face this time, it was everything. The way she walked, carried herself. It was her

STEVE: Her license forbids her coming here

REBECCA: (*pulling out her phone*) Look

STEVE: You took a photo?

REBECCA: As she was walking away

STEVE: You'll get yourself arrested

REBECCA:	Just look
STEVE:	(*looks at the phone*) Could be any woman with a ponytail
REBECCA:	But it wasn't. I'm telling you
STEVE:	Why would she be here?
REBECCA:	I don't know, I / don't
STEVE:	/ Ok, ok
REBECCA:	I followed her
STEVE:	What?
REBECCA:	I couldn't help it. I never thought I'd see her again and then there she was, plain as day, filling up her car. She drives a car. A nice car. A bottle green Prius. I watched her, fill it up, walk across the forecourt, talk to the man behind the counter. He laughed at something she said. She made him laugh and I thought 'if you knew…' Then she got back in her car and drove to a B&B in Scotstoun. (*Beat*) I got out of the car when she did but my legs wouldn't move so I just stood there in the rain with a pen in my hand… I don't know how long I was there for but someone must have seen me through the window cos the manager came out and asked if I was ok. I hadn't realised I was crying, he offered me a cup of tea. But I couldn't speak, so I just got back in the car and drove away. It was only

when I got home that I saw the blood... I'd
been gripping the pen so tightly my nails had
broken the skin

She opens her palm and shows him the cuts

Why should she be allowed to make people
laugh?

He touches her hand very gently

Is this justice?

STEVE: (*shakes his head*) Have you called the police?

REBECCA: They were very polite, said they'd check.
(*Beat*) It's all starting again

STEVE: No

REBECCA: I tell people every day that they have to find
a way to let go of the anger but when I saw
her, filling up her car bold as brass the rage

STEVE: I know

REBECCA: I'm a hypocrite

STEVE: You're human (*beat*) What can I do?

REBECCA: Stay with me. Tell me I'm not going crazy

*He holds her, lets her cry. Very gently he opens her hand, puts it to
his lips and kisses her cuts, she watches him. They look at each
other and he kisses her. After a moment they stop, it is awkward,
they laugh. She smiles, nods, makes to leave.*

STEVE: Don't do anything stupid Bec

REBECCA shakes her head

REBECCA: She's pregnant Steve

STEVE is paralysed.

SCENE 5

Same day. Mid-afternoon. Drumchapel. Hospital ward.
HAZEL, 58, sits in a wheelchair. She is wired to monitors and
has a drip. KAY enters, she is heavily pregnant, almost full term

HAZEL: It's you

KAY looks at her, nods

              Didn't know if you'd come

KAY: They said you were dying. Cancer

HAZEL: Aye. Riddled wi' it

KAY: I had no idea

HAZEL: No' something you write in a Christmas card

KAY: I'm sorry

HAZEL: Are you?

KAY: Course I am, you're ma' mother

HAZEL: And you thought you'd better have one last
              look

They look at each other

              Thought I'd come home to die

KAY: Because of all the happy memories?

HAZEL smiles wryly

HAZEL: Dangerous for you being back here, I'm
              honoured you took the risk

KAY is silent

HAZEL: It's been a long time

KAY: Aye

HAZEL: Did they tell you not to see me? When you got out? Did the psychiatrists advise it?

KAY: Some

HAZEL: I came to see you every week. Never missed a day, even when I wasn'ae well

KAY: I know. That's what you told the papers too

HAZEL: What does it matter what I said?

KAY: Half of it wasn'ae true

HAZEL: Everyone loves a good story

KAY: With you as the victim

HAZEL: Was I no'? I never brought you up to do what you did. No mother should go through that

KAY: And what about what I went through?

HAZEL: I was unwell

KAY: Is that what you tell yourself?

HAZEL: It's the truth

KAY: No, it's *your* truth. The things I did... at your bidding

HAZEL: Ma' mind wa / s

KAY: / Your mind was well enough to be heard in court

HAZEL: What did you expect? How could I defend you?

KAY: You could've told them that I could be gentle, that I wasn'ae born evil

HAZEL: But you were. A screaming, kicking ball of rage, fists clenched, red faced, no love in yer. I couldn'ae get near

KAY: I was a baby

HAZEL: I was afraid of you even then, didn'ae want to take you home

KAY: How can you say that?

HAZEL: Begged the midwife to keep you but tha said we needed time alone to bond (*she laughs*) I put you in the corner, waitin' for you to calm down so's I could hold you but every time I came near you'd scream louder

KAY: How can I be blamed for that?

HAZEL: You weren't normal. You were ma' cross to bear, ma punishment for lust

KAY: So you punished me from the day I was born

HAZEL: And you made sure I paid the price. You gave me a life sentence

KAY:	And ten thousand pounds for your story
HAZEL:	I had nothing else to sell
KAY:	Aye, I suppose your body wasn'ae worth anything anymore
HAZEL:	There she is, there's ma Kayleigh. Ma' Kayleigh Grey
KAY:	I'm no' her nae more
HAZEL:	You'll always be her. That monster inside you may be sleeping now but it's part of you, part of who you are
KAY:	No
HAZEL:	I wasn'ae a perfect mother
KAY:	You weren't a mother at all
HAZEL:	And there it is, that self-pity. We were all wading around in the shite but only you did that (*beat*) Does he know? (*Pointing at her wedding ring*) Your husband
KAY:	Course
HAZEL:	And he stayed?
KAY:	I'm goin'
HAZEL:	I thought tha's why you cut me off, so I wouldn'ae tell
KAY:	I cut you off because you're poison

HAZEL: Wha's his name?

KAY: What does it matter to you?

HAZEL: I want to pray for him

KAY makes to leave

> Got your fairy-tale ending, didn't you (*she looks at her bump*)

KAY looks at her

> But be warned. Fairy-tales teach us morals, good *always* triumphs over evil

KAY walks away

> (*calling after her*) The truth will out Kayleigh Grey

HAZEL recites the Lord's Prayer

SCENE 6

*The following day. Mid-morning. A bed and breakfast in
Scotstoun. KAY sits crouched beside the bed, she shakes violently.
The door bangs, JOHN enters*

JOHN:	What's going on?
KAY:	There's a car outside. It's been there all morning

JOHN goes to look

	Don't
JOHN:	(*gently*) OK, OK
KAY:	Someone knows
JOHN:	We don't know that
KAY:	I'm scared
JOHN:	It's okay, I'm here

KAY checks the window again

KAY:	Fucking hell. Fuck. I knew this would happen. I knew. What do we do?
JOHN:	We ring Sally. She'll send a car
KAY:	We cann'ae, I'm breaking ma' licence. We shouldn'ae have come back. Oh God. If they know what I look like. If they get a photo
JOHN:	Calm down

KAY: You go. This isn't your fault. If they get you
                as well

JOHN: Trace, calm down

There is a knock on the door. KAY is terrified

KAY: Leave it

JOHN: It's fine

KAY: Please J –

*JOHN exits to the door, KAY cowers in the corner. JOHN
returns*

                Who?

JOHN: (*proffering a piece of paper*) Receptionist, a
                note was left for you

KAY: No-one knows we're here

JOHN: The woman who left it had a photo of you, at
                the petrol station

KAY: Wha-?

JOHN: Receptionist asked if she should call the
                police

KAY reads the note, her breathing becomes distressed

KAY: It's her. Rebecca, Miss Hastie. She wants to
                meet

JOHN: (*protectively*) No

KAY looks at him

126

No Tracey, it's not safe

KAY is silent

JOHN: I'm ringing Sally

KAY: No. I shouldn'ae even be here

JOHN: You're not going

KAY: Don't tell me what to do John

JOHN: She could have a knife or a gun or other people, her husband... you think she just wants to talk, after what you did?

KAY is winded

        I didn't mean it like that, Trace, I just meant

KAY: I know what you meant

JOHN: I'm sorry

KAY shakes her head

KAY: What does she want?

JOHN: It's a trap

KAY: She was following me

JOHN: You don't have to go

KAY: Don't I?

JOHN: Why?

JOHN moves to the window

She's gone

Beat

KAY: What do I think I'm doing?

JOHN: What do you mean?

KAY: Having a baby

JOHN: We've been through this

KAY: IT DOESN'AE GO AWAY

JOHN: I know

KAY: I can still remember how she felt in ma' arms, the tininess of her body, how helpless she was (*beat*) her throat beneath ma thumbs

JOHN: Stop now

KAY: And I haven'ae met her yet but I love her, a love that fills ma whole body but when I think of it, it chokes me

JOHN: Breathe

KAY: What I did. How they'd 've felt when tha' saw her, when they heard what I'd done. How do they live wi' that?

JOHN: I don't know but it's done

KAY: What they felt because of me…

JOHN: You were a child

KAY: When I saw her in the court, she looked like a ghost, like all the blood had drained from her body and her bones had turned to liquid. He had to hold her up, her husband, but he wasn'ae much better

JOHN: Tracey

KAY: I wanted to say to her I was sorry but instead I stood in the dock, looked her in the eyes and told them all she didn't want her anyway, that she'd tried to have an abortion (*beat*) She broke down when I said that, let out this sob, everyone turned to look and she collapsed, like her body had just shut off. She didn'ae come to court after that

JOHN: You've served your time

KAY: Have I? No, no. Nothing I do, nothing will ever be enough

JOHN: So what then?

KAY: I can't keep her

JOHN is floored

It's no' right John

JOHN: Trace / y

KAY: / To let her be born into this. To belong to me

JOHN: No

KAY: What do I tell her? Or do I live in fear of her
              finding out who I am?

JOHN: She'll not need to know

KAY: No, no' when she's wee but when she's older?
              When she develops a mind, a conscience,
              when she reads about me in books, hears
              about me on the television or the radio? Asks
              me if I remember it happening, did I know
              her? What do I say? What do I tell her?
              Have I to carry this secret to ma' grave?

JOHN: We'll find a way?

KAY: How? How will I make her understand?

JOHN: Because you're not that person anymore

KAY: Course I fuckin' am (*beat*) That's who I'll
              always be

JOHN: Not to me

KAY: But to them, to Rebecca and Steve Hastie

Moments pass, they cool

              Is it fair? What I've done? Binding you to
              me forever. If I was strong I would've
              walked away, not left it to you. Then you
              could've railed and been angry but you'd
              have got over it, and when you had you'd
              have been relieved and found someone else,
              someone better

JOHN:	I'm not a child Tracey. I know exactly who you are and if I had my time again I would make the same choice. So don't tell me I'm too weak or too nice or whatever else to walk away because if I'd wanted to, I would have. (*Beat*) I'm not a stupid man and I'm not deluded. I know what you did. But I choose to see the goodness in you. Don't you ever wonder why I stayed when you told me? Why I wanted you to be my wife?
KAY:	All the time
JOHN:	Because the person I know would never do those things. You were robbed of a child / hood
KAY:	/ No excuses
JOHN:	And made the worst mistake and I will tell our daughter that
KAY:	It won't be enough. (*Beat*) They said I should be sterilised, signed petitions
JOHN:	They didn't know you
KAY:	No. But tha' knew enough.
JOHN:	But you were fourteen when you did it.
KAY:	I was a monster
JOHN:	You weren't. You told me, when you were in your cell you refused to close your eyes because you were terrified of wetting the bed,

so disturbed by what you'd done you were convinced Rosie was growing inside you. That's not a monster. Is it?

JOHN squeezes her hand

KAY: How can this be justice?

JOHN: Life goes on Trace. I want this baby

KAY: Oh John, I wouldn't ask you to give her up, I just can't do it with you

JOHN: So what? Do it on my own?

KAY: Or find someone else

JOHN: You're asking me to leave you?

KAY nods

KAY: (*gesturing to the baby*) For her sake. So she can have a normal life

JOHN: No

KAY: It's no' right

JOHN: Trace, it's your turn to trust me now

Another knock at the door

KAY: Oh God

JOHN gestures for her to stay calm. Exits to the door, returns

JOHN: (*gently*) It's your mother, Kay

KAY: Has she…? (*He nods*)

SCENE 7

2020. February. Two weeks later. Mid-afternoon. Drumchapel cemetery. HAZEL's funeral. KAY stands beside the open grave. In her arms she holds PHOEBE, 11 days old. JOHN stands beside her, his arm around her waist

JOHN: OK?

KAY: I didn'ae expect to feel sad

JOHN kisses her head

JOHN: Are you ready to go?

KAY: Few more minutes

JOHN: Do you want me to stay?

KAY: No, you go, I'll meet you at home

JOHN: You sure? Shall I take Phoebe?

KAY: No, I'll keep her with me

JOHN: OK

JOHN kisses the top of her head, exits. Moments pass

KAY: This is your granddaughter. She's nothing like you or me. She's beautiful and calm, just like her Da' (*beat, she looks at PHOEBE*). There was an old woman who lived in a shoe

REBECCA enters, she stands watching

        She had so many children she didn't know what to do, she gave them–

133

KAY realises she is being watched, looks up, gasps. They look at each other

KAY: You (*beat*) I'm no' ready

REBECCA: I couldn't wait

KAY tries to regain composure. Silence. They look at each other

REBECCA: I've dreamt about you

KAY: I'm so / rry

REBECCA: / Every night for nearly fourteen years. In my head holding my baby

KAY: Sorry

REBECCA: I didn't like anyone else holding her, not even Steve

KAY: I should take her insi / de

REBECCA: / But you didn't hold Rosie like that did you, they said she had bruises all over her body from the way she was carried

KAY: I /

REBECCA: / How can you be a mother?

KAY: I'm / sorry

REBECCA: / Is it allowed? Legally?

KAY nods, REBECCA almost laughs

REBECCA: Because you're rehabilitated? Fourteen years and the slate's clean. (*Beat*) You get all this

and she's in the ground wearing clothes she
didn't have time to grow into

A moment

Is it a girl?

KAY nods

Do you love her?

KAY: More than anything

REBECCA: (*fighting hard to keep it together*) Do you know
what you did now?

KAY nods

What you took? My most precious thing

KAY: I do

REBECCA: I could do the same

KAY nods, instinctively clutches PHOEBE tighter

What's her name?

KAY: Phoebe

REBECCA: Can I see?

*KAY cautiously shows REBECCA. REBECCA fights to keep
composure*

She's perfect

KAY: Sometimes I can't look at her. John has to do
it all

135

REBECCA:	Is that true?

KAY nods

	Can I hold her?

KAY is still

	I'd like to hold her
KAY:	No
REBECCA:	Please
KAY:	I –

REBECCA smiles, nods

REBECCA:	You took Steve as well
KAY:	(*distressed*) What can I do?
REBECCA:	Tell me you suffer
KAY:	It never goes away
REBECCA:	Good. Good. I'm glad. Because you see I can't believe in God, I've tried but... so I don't believe there's punishment to come, only what you get while you're here. And yet you've got (*she indicates PHOEBE*)

KAY nods

	But my Rosie never – (*beat*) Why her?

KAY shakes her head

	What did I do?

KAY:	It was ma' mind
REBECCA:	I need to understand
KAY:	I can't
REBECCA:	Steve blamed me
KAY:	No
REBECCA:	For trying to help... was he right?
KAY:	I – It wasn'ae
REBECCA:	Was he?
KAY:	No
REBECCA:	Tell me what you did
KAY:	No
REBECCA:	Why you did / it
KAY:	/ No
REBECCA:	I need to hear / it
KAY:	/ I ca / n't
REBECCA:	/ From your mouth
KAY:	No
REBECCA:	I need to know why
KAY:	You don't, it was pathetic
REBECCA:	Say it (*beat*) From the start

KAY: I'd been back from the foster family for a
week. Everythin' felt different. I'd been at
the pipes after school every day since I got
back, waiting for Zoe to come. Hopin',
prayin' she would. Then that day she did an' I
remembered why I was living, the reason I
hadn't got rid of maself. And then she told
me, told me she was pregnant by the boy
she'd been fooling with, that her Ma was
making her have it. She broke ma' heart. I
didn'ae know what to do with maself, where
to go. I didn'ae want to be anywhere, I
couldn'ae go home, she was ma home... and I
knew the only person that would care was
you. So I went to your house. I knew where
you lived, I'd followed you before, just to see.
And there you were, in the garden. I watched
you through the fence with Rosie, cooing
over her carry cot, all this love she was
getting. I just stood there drinking cider and
watching. Then I called your phone so I
could tell you to turn around and surprise
you. And then I saw you see my number and
cut me off. Not a second to wonder why I
was calling. And instead, you picked her up,
kissed her on the forehead. And I wanted
that, I wanted those kisses. So when you
went inside the house and left her I jumped
over the fence. I didn't know why. I didn't
know what I was going to do. But I wanted
you to see my pain, feel it. To punish you. At
first I thought I'd confront you and then I

saw her and I just did it. And even when I was back on the dirt track and I heard your screams I kept going. I didn't know I was going to... Ma mind was scrambled, I'd been drinking and taking pills. I called Zoe. Had this idea I could show her how good I was with babies. By the time I got to the pipes she wasn'ae even crying, just making this little gurgling sound

REBECCA sobs at the memory of that sound

She was so tiny, she didn'ae feel real. And then Zoe came and she didn'ae understand why I had her, started panicking, and I just wanted her to have fun and for me to be able to show her ma way wi' babies. And then she said she was marryin' Jack Harvey and I just, I took Rosie into the pipe and something went inside ma' head... beyond rage, beyond panic. Zoe was screaming and she was screaming and I put ma' hands around her throat and I started to press and I just kept pressing. And when I stopped she was still.

REBECCA: Was she scared?

KAY shrugs

Was she crying?

KAY nods, REBECCA sobs. They are broken

KAY: I'm so sorry

REBECCA looks at PHOEBE. Moments pass. Slowly KAY offers PHOEBE to REBECCA. REBECCA shakes her head, walks away

REBECCA: (*turning*) I'll never forgive you

KAY nods, watches her go, she is shaking

SCENE 8

Almost two years later. 22nd January 2022. 10pm. Drumchapel.
Down by the river with the tyre on a rope. ZOE, 30, enters. Sits on
the swing. Waits. Begins to swing dropping her head back. Stops.
Re-does her hair. Stands. Breathes deeply. Decides to leave but
before she does KAY, 30, enters. They look at each other

KAY: You came

ZOE nods

ZOE: Twenty-second hour of the twenty-second
                 day twenty-twenty-two

Beat

KAY: You turned into a swan

ZOE is embarrassed. There is an awkward pause

ZOE: I didn'ae tell anyone I was coming. Turned
                 around three times

KAY: Brave

ZOE: What?

KAY: Of you to come

ZOE is still

                 To see the 'monster'?

ZOE: What?

KAY: That's what you said in court

ZOE is silent

141

	That I was a monster
ZOE:	They told me to say it

KAY nods

KAY:	You wouldn't look at me
ZOE:	They said I couldn't
KAY:	But I looked at you. I never stopped looking at you
ZOE:	I know
KAY:	–
ZOE:	I could feel it
KAY:	I've still got all your letters from before

ZOE looks at her

	I never showed them
ZOE:	I thought you might
KAY:	Last thing you wrote
ZOE:	Don't
KAY:	I love you Kayleigh Grey. See you in the Isle of Muck
ZOE:	You ruined it
KAY:	You said you loved me
ZOE:	I know

KAY:	You were the only person who'd *ever* said that. The only person
ZOE:	I did. And you… because of me
KAY:	(*looks at her*) S'that what you think?
ZOE:	S'true isn't it?
KAY:	It wasn'ae your fault

There is a silence

Did you marry him, Jack Harvey?

ZOE:	(*shakes her head*) The baby died in ma belly wi' three months to go

KAY looks at her. Silence.

KAY:	I'm sorry
ZOE:	I was relieved

KAY releases a shaky breath

Could I have stopped you?

KAY:	What?
ZOE:	In court, they asked me why I didn't stop you
KAY:	You tried
ZOE:	That's what I said but they said I was bigger than you, could I no' have used my strength
KAY:	It wasn'ae your fault, it isn'ae your guilt

ZOE: I wasn'ae well for a long time afterwards, ma mind would play tricks. For a while I thought I'd done it (*beat*) Ma mam used to comfort me but I could see that question in her eyes, 'why didn't you stop her? I couldn'ae go back to school so we moved, changed our surname. The upheaval made her ill. She died a year after we moved. They all blame me, ma brothers and sisters, tha' don't say it but tha' do

KAY: I'm so / rry

ZOE: (*shakes her head*) / You've got your cross I've got mine

Beat

KAY: Are you making a life Zo?

ZOE: I'm tryin'

KAY: (*indicating her wedding ring*) Who is it? A he or a she?

ZOE: Mark

KAY: Mark?

ZOE: He's a computer analyst

KAY: No bleach then?

ZOE: (*smiles*) No.

KAY: (*teasing*) He sounds exciting

ZOE:	There was someone else, before, who was… but he wanted children and I… I could never (*beat*) Mark's older, got two sons from a previous marriage
KAY:	You'd be a lovely Mam, I always thought that
ZOE:	Too late now
KAY:	You're only thirty
ZOE:	I've been sterilised

Beat

KAY:	I've got a little girl
ZOE:	(*looks at her, shocked*) How?
KAY:	I tell myself I was someone else
ZOE:	Does it work?
KAY:	Only when I'm with her
ZOE:	What's her name?
KAY:	Phoebe. She's perfect
ZOE:	How old is she?
KAY:	Almost two
ZOE:	Are you wi' her Da'?
KAY:	(*nods*) Married me (*beat*) But it's always there, what I did, especially on happy days, there's always something that pulls me up,

145

stops me when I think what I robbed them of… it never goes. It'll never go away. And one day she'll have to know too and she'll judge me. Don't look at me like that. I deserve everything I get

ZOE: If I could give you one thing Kay, I'd give you back your childhood

KAY: There are countless unhappy kids out there who don't do what I did

ZOE takes her hand. They sit in silence

ZOE: Do you ever wonder who you might have been?

KAY: Sometimes (*beat*) I wouldn'ae be wi' a man

ZOE: Why are you?

KAY: Because he gave me a second chance. (*Beat*) 'Cos it makes me feel less like Kay, a choice she wouldn'ae have made. (*Beat*) And I wanted a baby. (*Beat*) You used to worship me

ZOE nods

ZOE: She's still in there, that girl. The bit of me that loved you. (*Beat*) And you've still got that look in your eye, the one that can make me do anything

KAY pulls up her top to reveal her chest. Stands on a rock.

KAY: (*shouting*) And I don't give a fuck

ZOE laughs

ZOE: Oh my God

KAY: No-one's looking

ZOE: No-one ever was. (*Beat*) I wish. I wish we could go back. To before

KAY: Can't have that, it's impossible

ZOE: Could I have made a difference?

KAY: No

ZOE: Who then?

KAY shrugs

KAY: I won't see you again will I?

ZOE shakes her head, KAY nods in response

ZOE: In a parallel universe

KAY: Aye

Pause. KAY smiles

We should just fuck off

ZOE: (*smiles*) Aye. To the Isle of Muck

KAY: We'll be savages. We'll eat carrots and dig holes if it rains. And ride the wild horses.

Lights fade

The End.